Tao
of puppies:

How to raise a good dog
without really trying

Krista Cantrell

THE LYONS PRESS

Guilford, Connecticut

An imprint of The Globe Pequot Press

10 9 8 7 6 5 4 3 2 1

Printed in the United States of America.

ISBN 1-59228-537-6

Library of Congress Cataloging-in-Publication Data is available on file.

Tao
of puppies

Dawn,

Have fun playing to
learn and learning to
play with your Welsh
Springer Spaniels.

Krista

Also by Krista Cantrell

Catch Your Dog Doing Something Right
Housetrain Your Dog Now

For Jeff,

who believes in my dreams and walks with me along a tao path.

Contents

Acknowledgments

The following people have my thanks and appreciation: W. Jean Dodds, DVM; Ian Dunbar, PhD, BVetMed, MRCVS, CPDT; John Fisher; Kathleen Fleet; Dianne Hahnloser; Cyndy Heisler, Hunter Heisler, Sage, and her puppies (golden retrievers); Tamara Huddleston and Callie (Cavalier King Charles Spaniel); Nina Lanphere, Ron Marchelletta, and Gidget (golden retriever); Mike and Jackie Murphy and Molly (Labrador retriever); Debby Ryan (Saint Bernards); Terry Ryan; Dr. Christine Stevenson; Debby Strieter; Wendy Volhard; Davi Volp; and JoAnn White.

A special thank you to a perceptive and gifted agent, Pamela Malpas, and a sensitive editor, Ann Treistman.

Many thanks and much gratitude to Ryan Harbage who believed in me and in my book, and helped me make it happen.

A heartfelt thank you to my pack mates: Jeff Cantrell, Red Sun Rising CD (golden retriever), Logan CD, OAP, OGC, OAC, NTC (golden retriever), Zoe Samantha AXJ, AX, OJC, OAC, O-NTC (Doberman pinscher), Pip AX, AXJ, EAC, OGC, OJC (border collie), and Jet Stream (border collie).

Photographic credits: Jeff Cantrell, Tamara Huddleston (pages 112, 153, and 211), and Kit Rodwell (page 65).

To contact me, visit my Web site: **www.kristacantrell.com**

Foreword

When I was thirteen years old, I read the *Tao Te Ching* (pronounced "dow day jing"), a Chinese manuscript from the sixth century B.C. that uses metaphors and embraces paradox to explore "tao," or "way," in eighty-one short chapters. In my twenties, I learned *tai chi* (pronounced "tie chee"), a Chinese martial arts form that I taught for fourteen years. My studies in *chi kung* (pronounced "chee gung"), the practice of breathing, circulating, developing, and directing *chi*, began in 1991. In 1998 I traveled to China to complete a three-year study in Traditional Chinese Medicine and qigong. Today, I continue my exploration into Chinese thought, medicine, and qigong with an eighty-eighth-generation, Jade Purity, taoist priest.

As a cognitive animal behaviorist and qigong practitioner who practices Chinese medicine with animals, it was natural that the ideas of each discipline interact. A golden retriever that I met at the animal shelter, when I was searching for another dog to add to our family, brought the relationship between taoism and dogs clearly into focus.

The red golden retriever puppy, the color of cinnamon, stalks the perimeter of the shelter cage. He sees me, spins like a top, and wheels in panic. As he turns and leaps, two brown eyes seek me out. Dog and person share the same space, but with two different thoughts. He wants to flee. I want to help. I face away, crouch on the floor, and wait. He approaches. A sniff and a lick and the puppy runs to the back of the enclosure. Three, four, five times he runs near me. Finally, he lands, settles, and lies close to my feet. We sit in silence. He sighs, shifts, and moves closer to me. I run my hand through his fur. And the silence grows and fills us. No longer empty inside, the dog's fear disappears. Twenty minutes later, we walk out of the enclosure together, and Red Sun Rising joins our family.

While schooling this hyperactive, previously abused, rescue dog, I learned that contrary to what most people believe, people don't train puppies, puppies teach people! Puppies teach us to delight in raindrops, walks, ball games, and to savor the bond that grows between friends. In the process, we can tap into our inner wisdom, reduce our stress, and share in our puppy's joy.

I work with dogs of all ages, sizes, and temperaments. In group classes and private lessons, shelties learn agility, boxers master obedience, whippets learn how to play with children, and puppies participate in "yappy hours." My day may start with a barky toy poodle and end with an aggressive German shepherd.

Currently, my family includes my husband Jeff, two golden retrievers, two border collies, a Doberman pinscher, an orange tabby cat, and five horses. Every year for the past four years, a new puppy has joined our family: first, a golden retriever; next, a Doberman pinscher; and finally, two border collies. They all walked a slightly different taoistic path. Each puppy stimulated my thinking and expanded my understanding of tao.

The *Tao of Puppies: How to Raise a Good Dog without Really Trying* results from my search to find the underlying principles that can be applied to any puppy, person, or situation. The *Tao of Puppies* goes beyond traditional training techniques to the source of creative power—tao. You learn how to follow the rhythms of nature, become an "intuitive silent trainer," practice the art of dog training, and raise a good dog without really trying.

The *Tao of Puppies* shows you how to flow with puppy energy, instead of fight against it. You discover how to subtract rules, not add them. The book begins by explaining how to create a relationship built on trust and mutual respect following the intuitive wisdom of tao. As the chapters unfold, you learn about the canine world, a puppy's nature and needs, and your role in raising a good dog. You find out how to create a special bond between you and your puppy. Then, you learn techniques for teaching your puppy good manners. The *Tao of Puppies* is not a conventional training book. Instead of training and obedience exercises, it shows you practical and fun ways to work with natural canine behaviors and raise a good dog.

The book is divided into five sections:

The first section, "The Way of Inner Knowing," introduces taoism. It explains how taoism applies to you and your puppy. It teaches you to "think like a dog" and see dogs in a new light.

The second section, "The Way of Skillful Living," helps you access your inner sense, pick a puppy that matches your lifestyle, create a safe environment, and grow a healthy puppy.

The third section, "The Way of Learning," teaches you how to become an intuitive silent trainer. It points out that when a puppy accepts you as leader of the pack, the puppy listens, changes, leaves, or stops what he is doing and complies with your requests.

The fourth section, "The Way of Practice," explains how to teach your puppy nine performance-pair behaviors that every puppy needs to learn: look/free, sit/down, take it/leave it, up/off, gentle/tug, bark/quiet, place/come, walk/stay, and outside/inside.

The fifth section, "The Way of Play," covers how to incorporate puppy raising into daily life. It explains how you and your puppy can have fun "learning to play" and "playing to learn." It describes games and activities that develop a confident, well-mannered dog, teach self-control, and are fun for you and the puppy to play.

Throughout the book, quotations from the *Tao Te Ching* are cited, to introduce, support, and describe a natural schooling process.

You do not need to travel to China or search for a sage to learn about tao. A puppy, "furry ambassador of tao," resides in your home and walks merrily with you down a taoist path. The *Tao of Puppies: How to Raise a Good Dog without Really Trying* helps you understand that teaching works both ways. You teach the puppy to be a good dog, and he teaches you to think like a dog, stop trying to force things, enjoy life, and keep hope alive.

Tao
of puppies

Part 1 | The Way of Inner Knowing

Chapter 1
About Tao

Tao existed before words and names,
before heaven and earth,
before the ten thousand things.
It is the unlimited father and mother
of all limited things.[1]

Grasshoppers, ants, pine trees, swimming pools, eggplants, and Lhasa apsos; everything is tao. Tao exists, soars, rests, and abides in all things. Tao dances in the wind. It resides in every stage of life from caterpillar to cocoon to butterfly. Unlike the butterfly, tao cannot be pinned to velvet backing and placed inside a glass box. Tao cannot be contained by any specific item, object, person, animal, or force of nature. It is endless, infinite, and without boundaries. No one can find *the* tao, because tao cannot be limited to an isolated object or solitary being. However, tao can be felt, experienced, and understood.

This paradox—that tao cannot be defined, yet tao resides in every cantaloupe, Gordon setter, and pencil—resolves as soon as we quit searching for tao with physical senses and use our inner sense to recognize a natural creative process. Although tao may be invisible to touch and sight, it can be experienced.

Puppies provide a perfect pathway to experience tao in our lives. Puppies, like tao, represent the unknown. We invite a total stranger to live with our family. We encourage a twelve-week-old poodle to join us when we water the grass, weed the garden, and visit our friends. We ask an eighteen-week-old shar-pei to drive with us to Utah, sleep in motels, and share our chicken sandwich.

Rosie, a fourteen-week-old, mixed-breed mutt, entered Gretchen's life when she was hit by a car in front of Gretchen's house. At the sound of squealing tires, Gretchen looked out her kitchen window and saw a small, reddish-brown body lying in the road. Without taking time to dry her hands from the soapy dishwater, she ran to the puppy. Two children were chasing a car, yelling at the driver, but Gretchen only had eyes for the furry body in the road.

Gretchen yelled for her husband, Bob, to find her. "A puppy is hurt. Hurry! I'm in the street!" Gretchen knelt down and saw that the tiny hazel puppy was breathing with huge irregular breaths that shook her shattered body. At that moment, Gretchen knew she would do whatever it took to keep the puppy alive.

Gretchen's decision to save the puppy's life revealed her true nature. To express your true nature is to know tao.

> . . . nourishing life,
> shaping things without possessing them,
> serving without expectation of reward,
> leading without dominating:
> These are the profound virtues of nature
> and of nature's best beings.[2]

At the emergency hospital, Gretchen learned the grim news. The puppy's body was covered with bumps and bruises. Her hip and bladder were badly damaged. The veterinarian said the puppy would require hip surgery to insert a metal plate. However, since the puppy was a stray, the veterinarian was required by law to send her to the Humane Society. Gretchen visited the puppy at the Humane Society three times a day for a week.

The staff at the Humane Society decided that the puppy should be euthanized because of her injuries and paralysis. Gretchen talked with anyone who would listen, pleading for the puppy's life. Finally, the Humane Society allowed Gretchen and Bob to adopt the puppy. They named her Rosie.

The next morning Rosie had hip surgery. Two weeks passed before Gretchen was allowed to bring her home. Her recovery was long and painful. Every time someone touched Rosie, it caused pain. She could not walk. Gretchen and Bob took turns carrying her outside, so she could eliminate. Rosie was alive, but her life was filled with pain and fear.

I met Rosie when she was six months old. Rosie was still afraid of Gretchen. If Gretchen tried to pet her, she would tuck her tail and run away. Rosie was scared to enter the backyard. If someone came to the house, Rosie would pant and run in circles around the dining room table. She could not relax until the visitor left.

We started simply. Gretchen and I sat on my office floor with our backs resting against the navy couch. We placed Rosie between us. I did not talk. I stilled my mind, opened my heart, and allowed tao to join us. My hands gently stroked Rosie's body searching for the tight spots where fear resides. My fingers released, soothed, and carried tao's message of unity among all creatures. Rosie's shaking stopped. She relaxed. During the car ride home, she napped.

After several placid sessions, Rosie raised her head, roused her body, and left our quiet sanctuary to explore my office. Now she was ready to learn "sit," "down," and "come"; perfect behaviors to help Gretchen learn how to interact with Rosie in a positive, nonthreatening way.

Eventually, we quit the safety of my office and moved outside to the agility ring. Rosie learned how to climb a five-foot-six-inch A-frame, run through a tunnel, and lie down on a table. Each session built on the previous lesson. As Rosie relaxed, she grew in confidence. Rosie's recovery demonstrated an important tao lesson. Tao runs, jumps, sits, and leaps; courage is really a verb.

Now Rosie greets Gretchen's parents at the door, trots outside to play in the backyard, heels by Gretchen's side as she pushes her son in the stroller, and holds her tail high.

Gretchen acted without thinking when she saved Rosie's life. It was a subconscious gut-level decision. She did not pause on that fateful day to debate whether aiding the dog was in her best interests. Without hesitation Gretchen ran to help an injured puppy lying in the road. Gretchen's spontaneous gesture of compassion expressed her true nature. Gretchen was thoughtful, unselfish, generous, and patient.

Saving Rosie's life cost Gretchen time, money, and sleepless nights. For months Rosie rejected Gretchen's attempts at friendship. However, uncluttered by expectations, Gretchen followed a tao path that allowed her to untie the knots that bound Rosie so tightly into fear and mistrust.

The impact of the hit-and-run lingered long after Rosie's emergency trip to the veterinarian. Random, senseless violence had made a stormy entry into Gretchen's life. No longer an anonymous face tied to a hit-and-run accident described in a local newspaper, Gretchen faced the violent destruction outside her front door, unmasked the victim, and named her Rosie.

The precipitous arrival of Rosie initiated Gretchen into essential taoist teachings: to help without expectation, guide without dictating, and honor life. By expressing her true nature, Gretchen experienced tao. When you experience tao, you can reclaim an inner wisdom that allows you to heal hearts, mend minds, and nurture life.

I met my first taoist sage in Trevor, a golden retriever. In the beginning, I did not understand why Trevor was content to let his actions teach me. However, his lesson was to show me the world without words, agendas, or plans. Because Trevor lived in silence, I listened with an inner sense and entered one of tao's hidden pathways.

I remember quite clearly one lesson that Trevor taught me.

The Ralston Purina red-and-white water dish moves across the kitchen tile, coming to a complete stop against my foot. Warm water sloshes against my left ankle. Trevor walks over to the refrigerator door and waits. Trevor likes cool water.

"No problem," I say. "Cool fresh water at your service."

I pour the warm water into the empty sink and set the dish on the floor. I reach inside the refrigerator for the green water jar with the yellow lid, unscrew the top, bend over, and pour cool water into his dish.

Trevor starts drinking. The opening of the refrigerator door spurs Red, the skinny, new, rescue puppy, into action as he leaps over a black plastic garbage bag that bars his kitchen entry. Sliding across the tile floor, he pushes Trevor's head away from the cascading water and drinks. Trevor's legs do not shift from their position. He does not growl, bark, or bite. Instead, Trevor waits. With Red's last greedy slurp, Trevor lowers his head and drinks.

Every day Trevor waits. Every day Red drinks first. Every day I watch. Five months pass.

Finally, I figure it out. It doesn't matter to Trevor if he gets the first drink or the last. It's a big dish, and there's enough cool water for both Trevor and Red. Pass the water, please; there's enough for everyone.

The sage has no set mind.
She adopts the concerns of others as her own.
She is good to the good.
She is also good to the bad.
This is real goodness.
She trusts the trustworthy.

She trusts the untrustworthy.

This is real trust.

The sage takes the minds of the worldly

and spins them around.

People drop their ideas and agendas,

and she guides them like beloved children.[3]

When your inner sense recognizes tao, you gain a new perspective that is not obstructed by anger, frustration, exhaustion, love, or preconceived ideas. Aware of tao, you reclaim an inner wisdom that prevents you from getting in your own way. Now you can easily teach your puppy to come, sit quietly for petting, shake hands, or go outside to eliminate.

Unable to see tao, I discover tao in dogs. If we follow their lead, we can enter a world where dogs are taoist sages and tao is a subtle energy that binds hearts and souls together.

Chapter 2
Yin and Yang

The unfolding of tao can be as big as a galaxy or as small as an atom. The concepts of *yin* and *yang* turn the universe, spin it on a dime, and give you change. Yin and yang ebb, flow, intermingle, and gather. A puppy who sleeps at your feet demonstrates yin. Yin is gentle, quiet, still, cool, soft, slow, delicate, and feminine. Yin puppies can be male or female. A barking puppy displays yang. Yang is strong, active, full, warm, hard, quick, and masculine. Yang puppies can be male or female. Understanding whether your puppy is primarily yin or yang helps you figure out the

Sit is yin.

Run is yang.

easiest way to teach new behaviors, change inappropriate habits, create games, and develop a meaningful bond with your puppy.

Puppies who "sit" display yin. Puppies who "come" demonstrate yang. Stay is yin. Run is yang. Yin and yang are opposites. As opposites, they define and complement each other: fast and slow, excited and quiet, or strong and delicate.

Yin and yang depend on each other. They are two sides of the same door. If you push, the door opens. When you pull, the door closes. Movement causes the door to open or close. In the same way, motion causes yin and yang to separate. However, yin cannot exist without yang, and yang cannot exist without yin. Together they form tai chi (pronounced "tie chee"), or unity.

Their image is symbolically represented in a tai chi figure, which is a circle divided by two curved lines. The two spaces, one dark and one light, indicate yin and yang. A small dot inside each swirl signifies that each force contains the presence of the other. Yin always contains yang. Yang

Puppies form a yin and yang during play.

Yin and yang in balance.

always includes yin. In constant motion, yin and yang grow, diminish, separate, combine, and begin new cycles. Yin becomes yang and yang turns into yin. The continuous give-and-take of yin and yang describes a process of change. The way you teach, play, feed, and love a puppy shifts the balance between yin and yang. You can pull out good behaviors, or push the puppy into undesirable behaviors. On a small scale, yin and yang explains how to raise a good dog. On a large scale, it accounts for how wolves evolved into dogs.

> The Tao begot one.
> One begot two.
> Two begot three.
> And three begot the ten thousand things.
> The ten thousand things carry yin and embrace yang.
> They achieve harmony by combining these forces.[4]

The evolution of wolves did not happen in a vacuum. The wolves felt the pull of people and it pushed some wolves to seek campsites, scraps of food, and human companionship. People and "wolf-dogs" united in a quest for food, comfort, and safety. As time passed, the yang wolf instincts, habits, and mannerisms were modified and blended into a new yin form called "dogs." From the perspective of the *Tao Te Ching*, the evolution of dogs may have happened like this.

Tao gave birth to one.
Wolves were one.
Wolves gave birth to two:
wolves and wolves with doglike mannerisms.
The two gave birth to three:
dogs bred other dogs.
And from the pairing of dogs came 10,000 dogs.
The 10,000 dogs carry yin and hold yang.
Harmony grows by uniting yin and yang.

The history of dogs includes the presence of wolf genes and attributes. However, the different combinations of yin and yang drive the future of the "10,000 dogs." Every puppy consists of her own particular blend of yin and yang. The amount of yin or yang that a puppy possesses shifts and changes as she matures. No dog is completely yang or yin. The balance between them alters, transforms, waxes, and wanes. However, the predominance of yin or yang explains why, in the same litter, you can find a shy cocker spaniel (yin) and an assertive cocker spaniel (yang). Understanding the interplay between yin and yang accounts for why an enthusiastic shih tzu exhibits bravery during thunderstorms, but displays timidity upon hearing a smoke alarm. To recognize yin or yang puppies, pay attention to their attitude and energy level as they run, chase, bark, chew, dig, and play with you, their littermates, and other family members. Is the puppy intense or laid-back? Sociable or aloof? Independent or needy? Energetic or mellow?

Yin puppies are gentle souls with even-tempered and easygoing dispositions. Active, but not frantic, a laid-back approach suits their quiet nature. Content to observe, they sit in your lap, at your feet, or on a couch. Their happiness does not require constant entertainment or stimulation. Mellow, reserved yin puppies may appear as shy, aloof, or fearful. Although they are curious, they limit their explorations to familiar territory.

Yin puppy.

Yin puppies depend on the people they love. They "need" you and follow you on your trips to the kitchen, great room, or bathroom. However, they have definite limits. If you walk to the storage shed at the far end of your property, they may follow you for a short distance. Then, they will turn around and head for the back patio. In the safety and comfort of the chaise lounge, they watch and wait for your return. If a yin puppy sees you playing with another dog, cat, or person and she cannot reach you, she may whimper, whine, or bark until you pay attention to her.

Never the most dominant puppy in a litter, they are usually submissive to their littermates. If you watch a litter of puppies eat, the submissive yin puppy gets edged out by bigger, stronger, yang siblings. During play, a yin puppy raises a front paw in a sign of deference. She lies on the ground while a yang puppy stands over her. Some dog breeds show more yin characteristics—for example, Saint Bernard, Newfoundland, soft-coated wheaten terrier, clumber spaniel, Maltese, papillon, pug, French bulldog, and bichon frise.

Yang puppies are brave adventurers. Living life at high speed, they run, jump, bark, and chew with gusto. Full of high spirits, busy, and intense dogs, an interactive approach suits their lively nature. Bold, independent explorers, yang puppies can be enthusiastic, boisterous, and rowdy, or, emotionally reserved and distant. However, one characteristic holds true: yang puppies have their own agenda. They roam the neighborhood if a property is not securely fenced. As adults, they need consistent daily exercise. Walking, jogging, working stock, or competing in agility, obedience, or flyball suits their high energy levels. Some dog breeds display more yang features—for example, standard schnauzer, cairn terrier, Dalmatian, Australian cattle dog, border collie, German shepherd, Australian shepherd, Jack Russell terrier, and Weimaraner.

Every breed contains individual dogs with different proportions of yin and yang. Two identically marked Brittany spaniels may have very different personalities. One Brittany may be gentle and even-tempered, while the

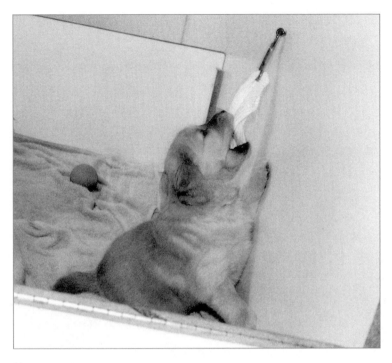

Yang puppy.

other Brittany may be noisy and hyperactive. This is true with every breed, not just Brittany spaniels.

As puppies grow, they learn, adapt, and change. You may bring home a timid yin pug, but because of your confidence-building work, she greets strangers happily and eagerly takes trips to the dog park. If an energetic toy fox terrier joins your family and you teach him an "off switch," he can learn to relax, take it easy, and not chase the cat.

All dogs contain yin and yang. Active puppies exhibit stillness. Fearful puppies possess trust. Quiet puppies embrace quickness. The next chapter, "Wu Wei," describes how following a tao path can help you balance yin and yang and raise a good dog.

Chapter 3
Wu Wei

Eternal Tao doesn't do anything,
yet it leaves nothing undone.
If you abide by it, everything
in existence will transform itself.[5]

A t first glance, the statement "Eternal Tao doesn't do anything, yet it
leaves nothing undone" sounds pretty exciting. Don't do anything
and raise a perfect puppy. What a smoking deal. And that's what it is,
smoke. There's no substance to the idea that puppies can raise themselves
without your input. Puppies need a pack leader who understands that although tao does not act, it is the source of every action.

The term *wu wei* (pronounced "woo way") describes actions that
occur without force, pressure, or stress. Wu wei does not demand—it allows.
A person who uses force insists a boxer "lie down." She holds onto a leash
and places her foot on the section of choke chain near the dog's neck. As
her weight bears down on her foot, it increases pressure around the boxer's
neck, and causes the boxer's body to sink to the ground. A person who understands wu wei recognizes that boxers love to eat. Instead of force, he
lures the boxer into lying down with a tasty piece of freeze-dried liver.

Wu wei works with a puppy's inner nature, not against it. Puppies love
to play, eat, run, chase, explore, and interact. If you recognize, accept, and
follow canine instincts, drives, and desires, you raise a happy puppy that
learns quickly. You don't get frustrated teaching the puppy how to "sit,"

"down," "come," or "roll over" because you follow the puppy's lead. Wu wei helps you join forces with the dog. No longer isolated in your efforts, you create a willing partner, friend, playmate, and pack member. The puppy readily responds to your requests because the puppy leads the way.

Wu wei operates without pressure, tension, and anxiety. You relax. Your inner sense awakens and you discover essential puppy wisdom hidden in canine cause and effect. You learn to take each situation as it comes, work with it, and not "get in your own way." Your respect for canine wisdom grows good behavior, increases a puppy's joy, and multiplies your happiness. By allowing, not forcing, puppies learn easily, and you experience tao.

Before I understood the concept of wu wei, house-training puppies was a chore for me and my husband, Jeff. Our dogs sleep on the floor in our bedroom. The advent of a new puppy requires that I place a piece of marine-grade plywood over one section of carpet, cover the plywood with newspapers, and wrap a four-foot-high, metal exercise pen, or x-pen, around it. At night I place the puppy inside the new den with a bed, toys, and a towel that smells like her littermates. In our house, Jeff has "night duty." He wakes up every two or three hours and takes the puppy outside to eliminate. Over the next ten weeks, Jeff's nightly bathroom wake-up calls decrease. Eventually, he sleeps through an entire night without interruption.

Sleepless nights were not a problem when we house-trained Jet, our 9-week-old border collie. Jet's breeder had taught her to eliminate in a litter box. We placed a plastic litter box lined with newspapers inside the exercise pen. During the night, when Jet needed to wet or poop, she used her litter box and then went back to sleep. Jeff did not have to wake up once to take her outside to eliminate. Easy? You bet. Understanding wu wei took the stress out of house-training Jet. We did not have to listen for restless movements or whimpers that meant she needed to eliminate. Instead, Jet house-trained herself. At night, we just "allowed" it to happen by providing a large x-pen, a clean litter box, and a puppy's natural inclination to separate where she eliminates from her sleeping area.

Jet in the exercise pen with a litter box.

During the day, we brought Jet outside and rewarded her for elimi-nating in the backyard. At night, Jet used the litter box. By the time Jet was eighteen weeks old, she no longer needed to urinate or defecate dur-ing the night. We removed the litter box from her x-pen.

By using a house-training approach that understood wu wei, we took the stress out of house-training, relaxed, worked with the situation, and got out of the way. (To teach your puppy how to use a litter box, see pages 225–27.)

When you get out of your own way, raising a puppy is stress-free and easy. However, if you demand too much of yourself, the puppy, and the sit-uation, you create problems and increase your anxiety and the puppy's discomfort—as Candace discovered when she attempted to teach Mason Dixon, a Portuguese water dog, how to swim.

Portuguese water dogs love to swim. Candace loves Mason Dixon and wants him to earn his water dog titles. When Mason Dixon is fourteen weeks old, Candace drops him into the swimming pool and expects him to swim. Frightened by his sudden arrival into the deep end of the swimming pool, Mason Dixon inhales too much water and plunges to the bottom of the pool.

Candace forces Mason Dixon to try to swim before he is ready. As a result, he sinks like a rock and almost drowns. Now Mason Dixon panics any time Candace brings him to the pool. A wu wei method of teaching swimming starts with Candace holding Mason Dixon in her arms as she sits on the top step at the edge of the pool. Mason Dixon feels the water lapping against his body and on his legs. Safe and secure, he leaves her arms to walk and sit on the step beside her. Exploration happens on his terms. The second day, Candace sits on the second step. Water covers Mason Dixon's back, but he experiences no fear. The third day, Candace holds Mason Dixon's favorite toy, squeaks it, and throws it a foot away to float on the water's surface. Mason Dixon swims to grab it.

A wu wei approach accepts that a puppy's physical and mental maturity affects his ability to listen, comprehend, and perform. Less-than-perfect behaviors are viewed as natural stages in development. Puppies only disappoint us when they are placed in situations for which they are unprepared. With wu wei as your guide, you nurture, grow, and direct a puppy's instincts, drives, and skills by understanding the canine nature.

Wu wei is the opposite of force. Instead, wu wei flows like whipped cream in a steaming mug of hot chocolate. It blends with the situation and makes us richer for the experience. People who adopt a wu wei approach apply insight, not compulsion.

You're busy. There's not enough time for you to work, wash the clothes, take the kids to soccer and baseball games, and raise a puppy. You force yourself to meet unrealistic demands and press the puppy to meet your expectations. However, force increases stress. It depletes your energy, increases frustration, and prevents you from successfully caring for the new dog. Before I figured out the wu wei method of house-training, my belief that house-training required frequent interruptions to Jeff's sleep resulted in more work and less rest.

Wu wei does not prevent a hectic day at work, bumper-to-bumper traffic, bouts with the flu, or children with measles. Instead, it helps you work *with*, not against, yourself and the puppy. You accept life's challenges and flow with them.

Two assumptions sabotage your efforts to raise puppies without stress. The first assumption: you control a puppy's behavior. The second assumption: learning happens in only one direction. You teach and the puppy learns.

THE FIRST ASSUMPTION: YOU CONTROL A PUPPY'S BEHAVIOR.

Puppies are curiosity-driven explorers, inventors, and experimenters. When Carson, the Airedale, bats a ball between her front paws, it improves her coordination. The climb to the top of the sofa teaches her balance and dexterity. Carson tugs on a carpet to test her strength. She chews toys,

Curious puppies explore.

bones, and sticks to build her jaw muscles. Her investigation behind closet doors leads to high-heeled shoes that create strong jaws; the hard leather softens as she chews them.

Puppies learn by doing. Their canine nature insists on it. Carson watches, studies, searches, inspects, sniffs, chews, barks, digs, and runs. As Carson explores, she learns, develops her skills, and figures out her place in the pack.

Dogs are not remote-controlled action toys. They think, process information, and learn. They make choices constantly. They must decide whether to chew a toy or eat the side of the couch; watch a bicycle or chase after it; or lie on the grass or dig a hole. You can ask, reinforce, teach, supervise, and develop behaviors, but the reality is, the dog decides. Carson controls her actions, not you.

However, you *can* teach Carson how to make appropriate decisions and practice self-control. For example, you can design schooling sessions

Puppies love to run.

that teach a puppy the difference between acceptable and unacceptable objects to chew. In the bedroom, place a puppy's favorite toy and a previously chewed shoe on the floor. Separate them by at least three feet. Then, bring the puppy into the bedroom. If the dog runs over to the toy, picks it up, or lies down to chew it, reward her with praise, food, or playing with the toy. If the puppy runs over to the shoe, tell her "leave it." Redirect her attention to her favorite toy by touching, moving, and playing with it. Praise the puppy when she leaves the shoe and grabs the toy. Repeat this technique in new locations with different acceptable and unacceptable objects and toys. Now, when the puppy is home alone, she can decide which objects to chew or leave alone based on information from previous schooling sessions. Chapter 20 describes in detail how to teach "take it" and "leave it."

Growing up is a puppy's main job. How high can she jump? How fast can she run? How strong are her teeth? Exploring and testing her body and environment causes a puppy to bark at cars, chase kids on in-line skates, run after squirrels, chew garden hoses, or sleep on soft towels pulled down from a bathroom towel rack.

Every experience builds puppies' senses of sight, smell, touch, movement, and hearing; influences their confidence; teaches them important coping skills; and develops their ability to test reflexes, skills, and knowledge. Only by chasing a cat can a puppy learn about cat behavior. Cats that run away and climb into trees or escape onto countertops reward the chasing instinct. Cats that turn, hiss, and swipe a puppy's nose with their paws teach a puppy respect and decrease the chasing instinct. Puppies learn about cats, children, visitors, garbage cans, and paper towels by interacting with them.

Physically, a puppy starts life deaf and blind and with limited mobility. However, changes appear soon. Eyes open at 13 days. Hearing develops at 19½ days. By 21 days, puppies start walking, upper teeth appear, and tails wag. At four weeks, their jaw muscles are underdeveloped, but sharp teeth make up for less strength. Nursing on their mother's nipples and playing with littermates teach them to bite softly.

During the first seven weeks of life, puppies usually live with their mother and littermates in a whelping box. Whelping boxes range from six-foot-square plywood boxes for a chow chow's litter, to a dresser drawer that has been placed in the kitchen for Pekingese, to elaborate metal-mesh

In the beginning, a puppy is born deaf and blind.

A two-week-old golden retriever puppy only weighs 2¾ pounds.

Weaning introduces puppies to solid food.

kennels for German shorthaired pointers. In this small, confined dog world, puppies develop motor skills and acquire knowledge that teaches them how to act like dogs. They figure out where to eliminate, how to play, and what to eat.

Knowing where to urinate or defecate is one of the earliest behaviors puppies learn. Between three to five weeks, puppies leave the whelping box to eliminate. By nine weeks, puppies leave the whelping box to eliminate in a specific place.

Pack dynamics begin at five weeks. Puppies now search for each other. By seven weeks, puppies react to a strange place and separation from their littermates by constant barking. At this time the final weaning from their mother also takes place.

Biologically, a puppy's brain is relatively mature at five weeks. By eight weeks, a puppy has an adult-like brain. This, however, is the physical structure. Mentally, a puppy is still a goofy fur ball.

The end of this first developmental period coincides with the time when many puppies arrive in their new home. The change happens in an

Golden retriever puppies in a whelping box.

Saint Bernard puppies in a whelping box.

instant. One moment, puppies are with their brothers and sisters. The next moment, they are alone. Puppies bark at night in their new homes because they are separated from their pack and in an unfamiliar place. Now, they must learn how to act like a dog in a human environment.

Wu wei cannot change the fact that a puppy barks when he is separated from you at night. Alone, in a strange place, he sleeps without his pack members for the first time. Instead, wu wei helps you understand the importance of pack. You prepare for a puppy's departure from his littermates by bringing to the breeder soft toys and towels for all the puppies to play with, sleep on, and chew. When you bring the toys and towels home, they carry the litter's scent and help the puppy with his transition to your place.

Wu wei reminds us to consider a puppy's nature when we invite him into our life. Understanding canine development helps you work with your puppy. By learning different aspects of canine physical and social development, how dogs communicate, and signs that indicate stress, you can encourage, guide, and grow your puppy's behavior. To put wu wei into practice, you need to learn, recognize, and understand normal puppy behavior. Puppies do not suddenly become dogs overnight. Instead, puppies progress through three social stages while they learn how to act like dogs in a human environment:

Stage 1. Puppy bodies, puppy brains.

Stage 2. Dog bodies, puppy brains.

Stage 3. Dog bodies, dog brains.

Stage 1. Puppy bodies, puppy brains.

Cute, adorable, eight-week-old beagles, bichon frises, and briards run, play, and cuddle with you. You know they are puppies because they must figure out where to place their feet when they walk up and down stairs. Do four feet land on a step, or two? Can the front feet move independently? It takes time for puppies to sort things out.

Puppies experiment with new things, test their bodies, and search for limits. They must decide whether or not to step on the new mat outside the back door because the prickly texture doesn't feel like carpet or grass. By twelve weeks, sight, hearing, touch, taste, and smell are fully developed. A puppy's barking increases or decreases depending on her environment. The same is true with separation anxiety. It disappears or worsens. Although puppies separate the area where they eliminate from the places where they live, eat, and play, they lack the muscle control to determine when it happens. Their bodies physically cannot "wait" to eliminate until they are at least fourteen to sixteen weeks old. To prevent house-training accidents, watch for obvious signs that a puppy needs to eliminate, such as sniffing, returning to a previously marked spot, scratching, or circling behaviors.

Between twelve to sixteen weeks, puppies play, fight, and establish dominance within their pack. Since they no longer live with their littermates, they work out pack dynamics with you and your family. During this time, they search for new areas to explore, such as closets, backpacks, and wastepaper baskets. They investigate farther away from home and may visit your neighbor's house. Increasing bladder and sphincter control help them wait to eliminate.

Throughout the first stage puppies look like puppies, smell like puppies, and act like puppies. Nothing misses their attention. An oven mitt tied to a handle on a kitchen cupboard turns into a new tug-and-release toy. Your son's open closet door invites the puppy to discover a gold mine of baseballs, in-line skates, and soccer shoes. The dog learns about her new home by searching, finding, and devouring. The sound of a doorbell initiates a barking, whirling frenzy. You think it's cute. New to your life, the puppy and you spend a lot of time together, and your expectations are low. You are a tolerant, benign puppy lover.

Stage 2. Dog bodies, puppy brains.

By week twenty-four, Karl looks at his puppy and sees a dog. Michelob, his Jack Russell, is six months old. Adult teeth appear. Bodies are bigger, stronger, and more athletic. At sixteen weeks, puppies are two-thirds of their adult size. At twenty-four weeks, puppies are similar in size and ability to adult dogs. During this time it is easy to confuse biological processes with mental and emotional maturity.

Karl loves Michelob. However, he does not understand why Michelob does not "come" when he calls him. He's tired of Michelob jumping on his legs when he comes home. Karl dislikes when Michelob barks when he watches basketball on television. During this stage Michelob runs out the door without Karl's permission, refuses to come when Karl calls him, nips at Karl's heels when he walks to the kitchen, and barks at him when Karl tells him to get off the couch. Unhappy, Karl thinks about locking Michelob in his crate when he watches television.

Karl has less time for Michelob, but Michelob needs Karl more than ever. The newness has worn off. Karl does not understand why Michelob doesn't obey him. However, at eighteen weeks, increasing testosterone can create feisty attitudes. In females, hormonal changes that occur around twenty-four weeks can cause anxiety, fear, and irrational behavior. Karl's frustration increases because he feels his control of Michelob slipping.

Between seven to ten months, many puppies enter a second fear period. Previously friendly, socialized dogs suddenly become shy, fearful, timid, or assertive. At this time, it's important to renew and redouble your socialization efforts with the puppy. Failure to work through this stage may result in an adult dog that is emotionally compromised. Seek professional help if necessary.

The second stage is an important time to remember wu wei and the influence that canine development has on behavior. Although a puppy's brain technically develops at eight weeks, mentally and emotionally, puppies are still immature. In many ways, they are a puppy in a dog suit. Instead of spending less time with Michelob, Karl needs to increase his efforts. The period from six to fifteen months is critical teaching, loving, and learning time.

Stage 3. Dog bodies, dog brains.

Amanda Devonshire, golden retriever, was my friend. I adored her. However, Amanda was a hyperactive, bouncy "puppy" until she was six. She and I went to obedience classes. We took walks. I worked with her every day, but like Peter Pan, she did not grow up.

Amanda had an electric personality. My thousand-watt dog. She taught me not to confuse the biological process of brain, bones, and muscle with mind, awareness, and self-control. Then one day a magical transformation happened. Amanda was still enthusiastic and full of energy, but she listened. She came when I called. She waited patiently at a stay. She walked without pulling and rode quietly in a car.

Will it take your puppy six years to become a dog? Probably not. However, dogs are not considered fully physically developed until they are two years old. Between the ages of two and four they achieve mental and emotional maturity. It takes time to raise a dog. Understanding wu wei encourages you to stay open-minded and kind. When you work with a puppy's inner nature, he accepts your guidance. When you pay attention to natural laws, you and your puppy live in happy harmony.

THE SECOND ASSUMPTION: LEARNING HAPPENS ONLY IN ONE DIRECTION. YOU TEACH AND THE PUPPY LEARNS.

It doesn't matter how smart you are if you
don't have the sense to honor your teachers
and cherish your responsibilities.[6]

Sometimes we get confused. We think our role as leader of the pack means we are the only teacher. However, we are wrong. The best teaching works both ways. With two teachers everyone learns faster. We learn from our puppies, and they learn from us.

We want dogs to teach us. When a puppy figures out that a specific behavior on his part affects our response, we have reached a significant turning point in our relationship. Now the puppy becomes a teacher.

At my house, puppies must be attached to a leash before they walk outside. Happy at an opportunity to go outside, Jet, our border collie puppy, waits at the door, leaping and bouncing in place. To snap a leash on a jumping border collie requires dexterity of eye-hand coordination and the ability to avoid a fast-moving nose-bounce to the face. I want Jet to learn that her actions influence my behavior. In the beginning, I ignore any bouncing and wait until she stands quietly. Jet learns the faster she plants four feet on the floor, the quicker I snap the leash to her collar and take her outside. Jet discovers that waiting quietly, not jumping, causes me to take her outside. At twenty weeks old, Jet sits quietly by the back door and waits when she wants me to take her outside.

Puppies teach us lessons that increase our awareness and ability to listen. We learn to look for a cocked ear, play bow, sit, or tucked tail—signals that tell us to pay attention now, something has changed. Puppies develop our curiosity as we wonder what they find so interesting behind the rosebush, or in the grass. They help us practice patience when we take them outside "just one more time" before we go to sleep.

Puppies increase our playfulness. We play hide and seek, toss tennis balls, and go for a walk in the woods. Puppies teach us that everything is an opportunity for fun: chasing a butterfly, sniffing flowers, and chewing a tree branch.

Puppies focus our attention and, if we are willing, help us discover tao's invisible pathway that connects our two lives together.

As teacher turns into student, and student changes into teacher, you and your puppy both get what you want: more joy and less stress. When

Playing ball with a puppy.

puppies become teachers, everyone learns. You realize that your behavior influences a puppy's response. The puppy understands that her behavior affects your reaction. Now it is easy to maintain the balance between what you want and what the puppy needs.

Wu wei recognizes that teachers come in all shapes, sizes, and colors. Playful Saint Bernards, happy Boston terriers, and enthusiastic Bernese mountain dogs show us how to raise a puppy without artificial rules, hostile environments, or rigid schedules. When we flow with nature, good behavior happens easily, without effort. The next chapter, "Effortless Effort," describes how to get what you want without really trying.

Chapter 4
Effortless Effort

We live in the high Sonoran desert near Phoenix, Arizona. Coyotes, owls, and rattlesnakes visit our property because it is horse-fenced, not dog-fenced. Our wood-rail fence leaves wide openings for furry and scaly visitors to enter. When I take a puppy outside to eliminate, he must be kept on-leash. No tightly woven fence keeps him safe if he goes out alone.

When a puppy first joins our family, I might take him out ten or fifteen times during the day. Instead of complaining about or resenting these interruptions, I use this time to school the puppy in bathroom manners and the art of walking on-leash without pulling. Our initial visit outside has one purpose: to walk to a previously marked area to eliminate. After I praise and reward the puppy for eliminating, we play "follow the leader" while we walk back to the house.

Most puppies run ahead and ignore the person who holds onto the leash. However, I want a puppy to recognize me as leader and walk quietly by my side. A puppy must learn that the "leader controls movement and territory." To teach a puppy to "follow the leader," I shorten the leash so a puppy can move in front of me only one foot, not six feet. If a puppy starts to run ahead, I stop, stand quietly, and wait. When the puppy reaches the end of the leash, he often tugs against it, but then he stops pulling. Most puppies look in front of them, around them, or anywhere but at me. However, I stare at a puppy's head and wait. Eventually, the puppy feels my gaze, turns, and looks at me. As soon as he looks at me, I move forward. However, if the puppy starts to run and pull in front of me, I again stop and wait until he turns and looks at me. During our many short schooling sessions from the puppy's frequent bathroom breaks, the puppy quickly learns to walk quietly by my side. It doesn't take any effort on my part.

Effortless effort is magic in action. Now you see it, now you don't. And what disappears is the struggle. Puppies willingly allow you to clip their toenails and give them a bath, and they will walk quietly by your side, "sit," "come," and "down." Effortless effort is the difference between "doing" and "being." I don't want to *do* something *to* my puppy. I want to *be* there *for* her.

Effortless effort is a process, not a goal. When you are aware of the process, desirable behaviors unfold naturally. You watch for the right moment to ask, allow, and encourage. You act. The puppy comes when you call because it's dinnertime and he's hungry. Every day you call "come." Each speedy arrival earns the puppy a huge food reward. By the end of the first week, the puppy hears "come," and eagerly runs to you. Problems only occur when you forget the laws of nature and confuse it with order, rules, and goals. Excessive focus on goals inhibits the natural process and often creates crises.

Trisha and Mel love their Yorkshire terrier, Tess, but training her is a nightmare. They complain to friends and family, even their dentist. "Tess is willful, disobedient, and constant trouble." Tess rummages through wastepaper baskets, drags pillows through the doggy door into the backyard, and nips at their heels.

Trisha and Mel both had dogs as children, but Tess was their first dog together. Mel remembered his family's German shepherd, Shep, who greeted him every day after school. Shep waited at the end of the driveway for Mel's return. They hiked, swam, and biked together. Shep never rummaged through the garbage or nipped at someone.

Trisha had fond memories of her springer spaniel, Maybell. Trisha dressed Maybell in scarves, hats, sweaters, and a feather boa. Maybell never destroyed her toys or ate a shoe. Trisha and Mel's memories did not prepare them for Tess. She did not match their childhood experiences of Shep and Maybell.

Trisha and Mel's goal is to raise a perfect puppy, just like Maybell and Shep. Instead, Tess chews the furniture, piddles on the First American rug in the dining room, and drags pillows into the backyard. When Trisha tells Tess to "stay," Tess ignores her. If Trisha pushes down on Tess's hind end to make her "sit-stay," Tess tightens her rear-end muscles and pushes against Trisha's hand. Tess wiggles and jumps. She rolls on the ground, but she does not "stay."

Trisha and Mel know what they want, but Tess does not cooperate. They think Tess is a poor imitation of Shep and Maybell. They reject Tess's feeble attempts to learn because she does not match their memories, dreams, and goals.

Trisha and Mel do not understand. They have specific goals for Tess: "sit," "down," "come," "stay," no chewing, and potty outside, but she does not achieve them. Raising Tess is hard work, and they are tired of it.

Trisha and Mel forgot that goals are the beginning of a process, not the end. Ask yourself, when you teach a puppy to "stay," is it the first step to a well-behaved dog or the last step? Trisha saw "stay" as a final destination. It was an isolated objective to achieve. Trisha thought Tess's refusal to "stay" was willful disobedience. She saw Tess's behavior as inferior-to-the-goal, rather than as a behavior-in-progress. Trisha did not understand that "stay" requires dogs to recognize a person as their leader, listen for the word signal "stay," understand what it means, respond immediately, hold a physical position without moving, ignore any distractions, and control any curiosity, eagerness, or excitement that might cause them to move.

When we ask dogs to "stay," they do not remain immobile for the rest of their lives. "Stay" is a temporary condition. After dogs "stay," they run, walk, or play ball. "Stay" is the pause between activities—a chance for puppies to rest, catch their breath, and pay attention. "Stay," or any behavior, is a circular process. In the same way, tao has no beginning or end.

Stand before it and there is no beginning.
Follow it and there is no end.
Stay with the ancient Tao,
Move with the present.[7]

Effortless effort requires that you understand that learning is a process. If you move with the present, and your vision is not clouded by preconceived ideas, memories, desires, or goals, you will see clearly. You will be in the right place at the right time. You will know what to do and how to do it. If your puppy sits crooked with one leg tucked under his hip rather than folded underneath to support his hips, you don't get discouraged. Instead, you realize that the puppy lacks the muscles to sit straight at this time. During the day, if you see the puppy tucking his legs under him in a correct sit, you praise him. If you have food or a toy with you, you reward him.

Understanding canine development helps you realize that the behavior you currently find so annoying will eventually disappear. With a minimum of effort, you easily shape a puppy's behavior with a word, touch, or sound. "Sit" happens, toenails are clipped, and barking stops. When you help, guide, and allow behavior to unfold naturally, you follow a tao path.

Chelsea and Howard practice effortless effort with Daisy, a Tibetan terrier. They also enlist the help of their friends and family to stop Daisy from nipping at their guests' heels. Effortless effort means Chelsea and Howard prevent Daisy's nipping without a single verbal reprimand. When people come to visit them, they ask their visitors to stand quietly and not look, talk, or touch Daisy if she runs up to them in the hallway or sniffs at their feet. Fifteen seconds pass. Daisy smells the guests' feet, but after thirty seconds elapse, she loses interest and leaves. With each person who visits, Daisy pays less attention to their feet. Eventually, Daisy ignores a visitor's feet altogether.

If Chelsea and Howard shouted at Daisy, hit her, or asked their visitors to push Daisy away with their feet, Daisy's nipping would escalate. Instead, Chelsea and Howard practice effortless effort. They understand that good behavior evolves, builds, and unfolds. Their guest's momentary inactivity discourages Daisy's interest in their feet.

Effortless effort is a process, not a goal. Focusing on goals narrows your perspective. Plans for tomorrow cause you to lose sight of today's progress. People who follow a tao path recognize that goals get in their way. A journey, not a destination, excites their interest.

Wise in the way of tao, you can participate effectively in a puppy's world with a minimum of stress. By adapting to the rhythm of a puppy's life, you maximize your relationship and minimize your efforts. Without really trying, you make a big difference. Puppies and people learn easily without stress or strain.

Raising a puppy is an adventure best experienced with laughter. The best teachers giggle, chuckle, snort, or hoot. They play games, toss a ball, sit in the grass, and give a food reward to motivate, teach, and encourage their puppy's behavior. Remember, if you are not having fun, neither is the dog.

A sense of humor saves me when I find myself chasing my puppy out the back door in my blue flannel nightgown and purple ski jacket. At the same time, the UPS delivery man arrives. Then, my neighbor sees me in my nightgown, ski jacket, bare legs, feet in slippers, and he stops to chat. The puppy, held tight in my arms, licks my face and tries to climb over my shoulder. Too silly for words, I smile and laugh at myself, the day, and this latest adventure. I'd go crazy without puppies teaching me to let go, relax, don't be so serious, enjoy life, and play. The perfect antidote to unexpected events and lifestyle challenges is the ability to laugh at yourself and the antics of your puppy.

Start by laughing; your puppy will love you for it.

Chapter 5

Unlearning Leads to Inner Wisdom

At a party, twenty people will have fifty different ideas about how to raise your puppy, plant your garden, and mend your love life. Everyone has an idea, or two or three, about what you should do. Your best friend says, "But if you only jogged with the puppy . . ." Your father reminds you that "When I had a hunting dog, I always . . ." Friends, relatives, and meter readers have suggestions to help you. You try their advice, read books, watch a dog-training video, and stuff your head with ideas, facts, and figures. However, you discover that when the crunch comes and your puppy begs at the table, you don't know what to do. Where are the experts? Not sitting at the kitchen table while your toddler flings his Cheerios on the floor. Your puppy races to eat each tiny little "o" before it hits the ground. Your son giggles and flings another spoonful. You don't know what to do—it's raining Cheerios, and you've got the blues. Whose advice should you follow? This chapter answers that question. But first, you need to unlearn.

We know how to learn. That's easy. Add facts, a generous helping of history, mathematics, language, sociology, biology, and a dash of discipline, and we are educated. Full of ideas and opinions that may be inaccurate, outdated, overly optimistic, the latest fad, or the truth, our knowledge comforts us. In spite of the things we know, or maybe because of them, we cannot figure out what to do with our fourteen-week-old Maltese.

Having little, you can receive much.

Having much, you'll just become confused.[8]

When your briefcase is crammed with papers, your pockets are filled with plastic poop bags, and your head is stuffed with deadlines, expectations, and plans, it's time to unlearn. Unlearning requires that you reverse, erase, undo, or break rules and preconceptions that limit your ability to raise a puppy and access the inner wisdom of tao. Unlearning makes you smart, open, vulnerable, and spontaneous. With fresh eyes and a quiet mind, you access inner wisdom. You realize that if you place the puppy in his kennel while your son eats breakfast, the incentive for airborne Cheerios vanishes.

Unlearning requires that you determine the ideas that prejudice your thinking. Beliefs such as "my setter mouths me because he's male," "terriers always bark," or, "collies always chase cats," prevent you from raising a good puppy. A single-minded belief that you have the right answer creates confusion, frustration, or dismay when your puppy doesn't do what you want. Locked into an idea, you lose the ability for inner knowing and do not experience tao.

I met Darlene and Misty, her silky terrier puppy, on a hot, sunny day in August. I drove fifty-five minutes through freeway traffic, fifteen minutes on four-lane biways, and five minutes skirting potholes on dirt roads to reach the townhouse complex at the base of a mountain in Mesa. A long trip for an appointment with a sixteen-week-old puppy.

I knocked on the door. The woman who answered had one cuff of her long-sleeved, blue, checked shirt pushed up to her elbow. The other cuff hung open at her wrist. Wisps of dusty brown hair fell in front of her small, pale gray eyes and curled loosely around her neck.

"You must be Krista. I'm Darlene. Come in. As you can see, we're painting." Drop cloths covered the furniture, a ladder rested against one wall, and paint cans were stacked in the hallway. The red Mexican tile floor had a trail of fresh, tiny, almond-shaped paw prints along one edge.

"We can talk about Misty in my bedroom," Darlene said.

I sat on a chair next to the bed and waited. Darlene returned with a tiny teacup terrier in her arms. As she crossed the threshold into the bedroom, Misty jumped down. She ran to a bookcase across the room and leapt to a shelf where a small row of paperback books created a smooth, open platform. Misty stretched across them. She tucked her front paws under her body and stared at me with bright brown eyes.

"This is Misty," Darlene said. "She's my baby and I love her. I haven't taught her anything yet. She's just a puppy." Darlene thinks Misty is too young to learn, but Misty knows differently. As Darlene answers my questions about Misty, I realize that Misty has already learned a lot. When Misty barks, Darlene picks her up. If she tugs on Darlene's shoelaces, Darlene stops and plays with her. As days pass, Misty barks more and jumps on Darlene and her friends.

"I asked you here because I'm confused. I love Misty, but she doesn't do what I want."

Darlene pampers, cuddles, and indulges Misty because she loves her, and Misty is "only a puppy." Darlene's attitude toward Misty emotionally paints herself into a corner because she believes Misty is too young to learn.

As we talked, Darlene realized that Misty started learning from the first day she entered Darlene's life. Darlene recognized that her responsibility was to work with Misty so she could learn the skills she needed to be a happy, good-mannered dog in Darlene's family. During the next six weeks, Misty learned to walk quietly on a leash, "come," "sit," "down," stop barking, and quit tugging on Darlene's shoelaces.

Darlene practiced "unlearning" when she altered her idea that Misty was too young to learn. As a result, she had an attentive, well-behaved puppy in six weeks. What you think affects what you do. If you want to experience tao and the inner knowing that flows with it, you need to unlearn.

Unlearning expands your understanding, helps you discover new teaching techniques, and changes your relationship to a dog.

In the pursuit of Tao,

every day something is dropped.[9]

Unlearning helps you reestablish contact with what is happening right now. If you want to shatter preconceptions, dissolve old habits, reveal patterns, and promote fresh ideas, three actions can help you. You can exchange minds, investigate options, and change positions.

Logan and the water bowl.

EXCHANGE MINDS: THINK LIKE A PUPPY

With five dogs in our house, we have large water bowls. A friend of mine, a potter, designed a brown ceramic bowl that spirals fifteen inches across and four inches deep to quench the thirst of my desert dogs. Its purpose is obvious: it holds water. That's my opinion. However, Logan thinks it's a swimming hole designed just for him. His nose dives under the water, front feet leap in, and he splashes. Geysers of water drench the tile floor, kitchen cupboards, and Logan. Puppies and people can look at the same situation in two different ways. That's why you need to "exchange minds" and think like a puppy. Then, you can understand that you fill a bowl with water to give life. Puppies use water to celebrate life. Smiling, you reach for the towels because you know that soon, the puppy will outgrow his "swimming hole."

Puppies see things differently than you do. Hats increase the size of a person's head. Sunglasses hide a person's eyes. When a tall creature bends down to touch a puppy with seven-inch hands, puppies cower or run away. Hats, sunglasses, and hands appear large and distorted to small puppies, which is why they often pull back in alarm, bark, or hide when a "stranger" appears. To reduce a puppy's anxiety, ask "strangers" to remove their hats and sunglasses when they meet your puppy. Request that they bend their knees and kneel next to the puppy, instead of bending over and towering above the dog as they reach out to pet her. After the puppy meets and greets them, hears their voice, feels their touch, and enjoys being near them, they can put on their sunglasses and hat while they interact with the puppy.

Puppies are sound-sensitive. Noises that we take for granted, such as dishwashers, garbage disposals, or trash mashers can cause puppies to pull back in alarm. They don't know what to expect. The vacuum appears harmless when it stands still, but as it rolls toward them—lights on, bar beating the rug—most puppies run away to hide in crates, under beds, or in another room. From a puppy's perspective, the noisy machine springs to life, disturbs their peace, and chases them. Suddenly, nowhere is safe.

To decrease a puppy's stress, associate something pleasant with a sound. For example, when you turn on the dishwasher, give the puppy a special food treat when it starts. You can also increase the amount of space between the puppy and a noisy machine. Trash mashers are not very frightening when puppies hear the noise in the living room, instead of in the kitchen. Gradually, decrease the distance between the scary sound and the puppy, until eventually the puppy can stand next to the trash masher, hear it crunch glass, ignore the noise, and eat a dog biscuit.

Exchanging minds keeps us fresh, curious, unassuming, and prepared. It raises our awareness, opens us to new ideas, and promotes better understanding between us and our puppies. The ability to understand what our puppies think helps us see in different ways, teach new behaviors, solve problems successfully, and not get stuck in old habits.

INVESTIGATE OPTIONS: SEARCH FOR THREE "RIGHT ANSWERS"

My grandmother always used to say, "There's more than one way to peel an apple." She used a potato peeler or a knife or an apple corer to pare off an apple's skin in a perfect spiral. Grandmother knew three ways to peel apples. Depending on the type of apple, she used a different method. In the same way, sometimes we need "another right answer" when we raise puppies. When we have more options to choose from, we make better decisions.

I know puppies can learn how to "sit" using a variety of techniques. One technique involves luring a puppy into a "sit" with a piece of food. By holding a piece of cheese over the puppy's head, and moving it toward his hindquarters, the puppy sits. If puppies are not food-motivated, balls or toys can also lure the puppy into position. Another method uses a sound to mark the exact moment that a puppy sits, and pairs it with a food reward. A third technique requires that every time a puppy "sits" during the day, you say "sit." As days pass, the puppy associates the word "sit" with the act of sitting. Three ways to teach sit, and all are correct. The technique to use depends on the puppy.

Finding three right answers is easy. If you think you know what to do, keep looking. Tao is everywhere. When you don't settle for your first idea, you start the unlearning process. The best answer may not be your first idea; the dog jumps and you knee her in the chest. Ouch. It's time to search for another way to prevent jumping. One option is to teach the puppy to "sit." Then, you can say "sit" and she cannot jump on you because her hind end is planted firmly on the ground. Or, keep the puppy in her doggy den when guests arrive. Then, she cannot run and jump on them. A third alternative is to lean your upper body forward in a body block. Do not ram the puppy. Leaning over and toward the puppy creates a more imposing figure that inhibits a puppy's desire to jump. A fourth choice is to drop down and greet the puppy on her level. Then, the puppy will not need to jump to greet you. There are many ways to prevent jumping.

In the beginning, you may feel perplexed, puzzled, stumped, or clueless as you search for three right answers. It's easy to feel at a loss if you think there is only one right technique or idea. To encourage new ideas, brainstorm. Condense your problem into fewer than seven words. Now, search for a solution. See what enters your mind. You can write it down, speak into a tape recorder, or tell a friend. If you brainstorm with other people, invite them to listen and contribute. However, they cannot shoot down any idea, no matter how ridiculous it appears. You don't know where an idea might lead. In brainstorming, there is no wrong answer. Some answers may not be workable, but they can stimulate other ideas. Later on, you can evaluate an idea's strengths and weaknesses. You can compare it to other ideas. Brainstorming is the time to explore.

If you cannot think of any ideas, name three things you see in the room or out the window. Figure out how they can be used to solve your problem. For example, you see a large magazine and think, If I hold it up, the dog can't see my lap if she jumps. It creates a barrier between us. The puppy makes the decision not to jump. My hands don't push her away and my voice doesn't say "no"; a perfect tao teaching technique.

In your search for three right answers, tao appears. Your inner vision expands and you see beneath the surface of first thoughts. Ideas straight from tao answer your questions, solve any problems, and create solutions.

CHANGE POSITIONS: LOOK AT A SITUATION FROM A DIFFERENT POINT OF VIEW

Four fingers folded against the palm of a hand. Thumb held tight against the second knuckle of an index finger. You see a fist; I see a sanctuary. Let me explain.

A dark triangular shape catches my attention. I stop writing. A dusky, mottled brown moth moves across the window that forms a barrier between my air-conditioned office and the warm desert air. The moth searches for a way to get to the sunshine, flowers, and trees, but a solid pane of glass keeps him inside. *Trapped.* Without hesitation I walk up to the window. My hand reaches out to catch him. His wings beat furiously against the glass at my approach. My hand freezes in midair. In a soft, low voice I say, "I won't hurt you; I want to help you get outside." His wings stop their frantic beating. Motionless, he waits. I cup my hand around him and carry him outside to a flowering paloverde tree. I open my hand, expecting him to fly away immediately. He stays. Explores. Softly waving my hand, I gently set him free.

Sometimes people act just like moths. Trapped by preconceived ideas, they cannot reach what they want. However, if you practice changing positions, you can figure out what needs to be done and how to do it. When you are confronted by drooling dogs, wet paws, or half-eaten toys spread across the living room floor, alter your outlook.

A friend of mine who raises Saint Bernards calls dog drool "icicles." However, changing positions is more than a word change; it's an idea change. Your stance changes because your focus shifts. For example, drooling is what stimulated Ivan Pavlov's interest in conditioned reflexes.

Pavlov knew that dogs drool if they have loose, floppy skin around their mouth that allows saliva to slip out. He saw his laboratory dogs drool and wondered why. He changed positions and looked for a stimulus that caused the laboratory dogs to drool. He found it. The people who fed the dogs every day wore lab coats. The dogs started drooling when they saw lab coats, not food. The lab coats stimulated their drooling. Slobbering dogs inspired Pavlov to change positions. He looked at drooling from a different direction, and spent the rest of his life studying the formation of conditioned reflexes.

In the same way, the wise person
puts himself last,
and thereby finds himself first;
Holds himself outside,
and thereby remains at the center;
Abandons himself,
and is thereby fulfilled.[10]

Think about raising a puppy as taking two trips. One journey leads you to explore the outer world. The other journey directs you inward. Exchanging minds, investigating options, and changing positions help you unlearn. In your trip, you discover that knowledge is not intelligence. Intelligence is not common sense. Common sense is not inner wisdom. Unlearning asks you to search for simple truths. No longer stuck in one way of looking at the world, you access inner wisdom and walk a tao path—and the puppy leads the way.

Chapter 6
Empty Mind, Full Intuition

In the space between waking and rising one morning, I lay quietly without thinking. After ten minutes, my mind rested on our sixteen-week-old Doberman pinscher, Zoe Samantha. Following an inner prompting, I realized it was time for Zoe Samantha to take her first trip to the bank. Dobermans are naturally reserved with strangers. At our local Bank of America, Zoe would meet friendly tellers who would pet her, smile, and make a fuss over their newest "client." Before we left, the bank receptionist—who stores biscuits under her desk—would give her a treat.

Upon waking, I did not debate the merits of the correct time to introduce a puppy to strangers and places. I was alert, but my mind was "empty." Minds are like busy market streets along the quay. Fish sellers unload boats. Dock workers load trucks. Vendors fill empty wooden tables with flowers, fruit, and fish. Casting its line, your mind searches for the catch of the day and grabs it. Emptiness removes the hooks, releases the fish, and your thoughts swim away. An empty mind contains no worries, wants, memories, or daydreams. Mental activity ceases and your mind opens. Receptive to tao, you "intuit" what to do.

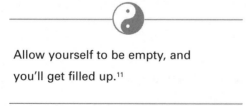

Allow yourself to be empty, and
you'll get filled up.[11]

An empty mind helps you experience the subtle knowing of tao pathways. By reducing the constant chatter in your mind, new sensitivity, insights, and hunches appear. Confusion decreases and awareness increases. If a puppy's behavior frustrates, angers, or depresses you, and you cannot figure out what to do, stop. Empty your mind. An empty mind enables you to understand what was previously hidden that kept you from successfully teaching your puppy or solving problem behaviors. You act and react in new ways as you teach, motivate, reinforce, and reward your puppy.

One way to empty your mind is to practice the following exercise. In the beginning, you may experience only fleeting moments of an empty mind. Expect it. Minds are busy places. However, with practice, emptiness grows. Start with five minutes. Gradually increase the amount of time you practice. The optimum practice time depends on your schedule. Do not force it. You can practice five minutes once a day, or three times a week. It's up to you. Start by practicing in a tranquil place. However, as your comfort level increases, you can practice anywhere: at a café, riding a bus, during a walk, or while grooming your puppy.

How to Empty Your Mind

Step 1. Find a quiet space where you can be alone.

An ideal time occurs after you wake up in the morning. Relax. Feel your body sink into the mattress. Or, sit outside. Rest your back against a tree, or sit in a chair. Do not lean against the back of a chair. Sit upright without straining to be vertical. Place your feet flat on the ground.

Step 2. Whether lying down or sitting, breathe with soft, steady, long breaths.

Close your eyes. Inhale through your nose. Follow your breath as it travels down your windpipe and fills your lungs. Feel the lower part of your lungs expand down and the upper part of your lungs expand up.

Exhale through your nose. Feel your lungs contract. Follow your breath as it leaves your lungs and returns through your windpipe and exits through your nose.

Notice how each inhale and exhale causes your shoulders to rise and sink from the motion of your breathing.

Step 3. Move your awareness to the space between the inhale and exhale.

Allow the emptiness of the space between two breaths to fill your mind.

Step 4. Breathe naturally.

Feel your body and mind rooted in emptiness. Pause. Don't expect inner knowing—just breathe. Wrap yourself in silence. In silence's rich, loamy soil, tao grows.

A return to silence rids you of emotionally charged reactions and brings clarity of thought. As insight grows, intuition increases. Now you can discover the hidden messages that impact chewing, mouthing, jumping, and digging. In silence you watch your seventeen-week-old Belgian sheepdog play with her toys, interact with your neighbor's rottweiler and Abyssinian cat, greet Great-Aunt Maud, and chase balls. You pay close attention to the significance of a curled lip, wagging tail, raised hackles, high-pitched bark, or play bow. As you focus on the Belgian's behavior, your sensitivity to a natural flow of events increases.

Sara has a six-month-old dachshund, Harry, who wets in the house at least two or three times a week. At first, Sara accepted that Harry's accidents occurred because he could not reach the doggy door in time. However, Sara knows that at six months Harry has the muscle and mind control to wait to eliminate until he runs through the doggy door to the backyard. Instead of blaming Harry, Sara sits in silence.

One afternoon Sara realizes why Harry has accidents in the house. In order to reach the doggy door in the bedroom, Harry has to walk by two, older, grumpy Akitas who sleep on the tile floor in the hallway. Harry refuses to pass them. This prevents him from using the doggy door in the bedroom, so he wets on the living room carpet. After Sara adds a second doggy door in the kitchen, Harry immediately stops wetting in the house.

Sara's use of silence emptied her mind and allowed her to access her intuition. As a result, she uncovered the common thread that bound Harry and the Akitas' behavior together. A cluttered mind interferes with intuition. Intuition grows in silence. Silence directs your attention inward.

Knowing what to do and acquiring a natural feel for timing relies on developing your inner sense. Then you can easily decide when to introduce your puppy to banks, hardware stores, or parks. You will know where mouthing ends and biting begins, and what to do about it. Intuitive pack leaders recognize that the Italian greyhound does not *lie* in her bed, but *hides* in her bed at the approach of the new pet sitter.

You don't lose when your mind empties—you gain. Your ideas expand. Newly awakened intuitive skills give you greater insight into the laws of canine cause and effect. Now when you decide to trim a puppy's nails, teach her to jump in the back of the car, or pick up her toys and put them in a box, you use your inner sense to direct your efforts. Intuition is more than a "hunch." Instead, inner stillness and outer events merge into one. No longer separate, intuition flows. With little effort on your part, you guide the puppy's behavior.

One evening when I walked Zoe Samantha on-leash to the "bathroom area" in our backyard, I learned the value of intuition in house-training puppies. I stood quietly while Zoe Samantha walked under the trees searching for the perfect spot to eliminate. In fewer than thirty seconds, she pooped. After a pile, I usually take a puppy back to the house immediately. One large pile for a little puppy is a big accomplishment. That evening I waited. Was it the lift in her tail as she finished squatting? I don't know; but my intuition was rewarded. Forty-five seconds later, Zoe Samantha pooped again.

Intuition works in big and small ways. It bridges the divide between puppy and person, behavior and instinct, action and reaction. Instead of feeling confused, upset, or defeated from too little information or too many choices, intuition asks you to accept small knowings from tao.

Everyone has the ability to experience intuitive tao pathways. The first step requires that you empty your mind and experience silence; then, ideas, emotions, or plans will not prevent you from accessing intuition. When your inner sense unblocks, opens, and expands, your sensitivity, insights, and hunches increase. Then, you can sense what was previously concealed.

The second step involves paying attention to details. Does the puppy bark because she's locked in a crate, sees a cat, or has hurt her paw? As awareness grows, perception expands. Intuition enables you to make the connection between what is obvious and what is hidden.

The third step asks you to have faith in your intuition. Tao flows on an intuitive wavelength. Paying attention to intuition helps you make better decisions. Trust it. You won't regret it.

Chapter 7
Intuition Works Both Ways

April O'Nealey's husband, Jim, is a member of a submarine crew. At sea for approximately six months, Jim never tells April when he will return home due to security precautions. However, April always knows when Jim sails into port. One day before the submarine docks, their bulldog, Kelsey, waits by the front door and refuses to leave.

Kelsey's behavior is a striking example of intuition. Intuition is more than seeing, feeling, or thinking; it is another way of knowing. Linked into tao, you rely on what you cannot see. Kelsey doesn't see or hear Jim. She senses his presence and waits patiently by the door.

In far less dramatic ways, puppies use their intuition every day. Fletch, Mac's twenty-two-week-old Labrador retriever, nuzzles his hand and licks him when he comes home tired from a difficult day at work. However, Fletch greets him at the door with a ball in his mouth if Mac's day passes smoothly. Fletch knows before Mac enters the house how Mac feels. Jenna, an eighteen-week-old Pekingese, hates going to the dog groomer. She hides in a closet one hour before her grooming appointment. Marie's fourteen-week-old standard poodle, Cannon, stops automatically and sits when Marie halts during their on-leash walks in her backyard. Before Marie comes to a complete stop, Cannon sits. Cannon anticipates Marie's intention to halt. Their backyard walks have turned into a game. Marie tries to fool Cannon. She walks four steps and stops. Runs eight strides and halts. Marie skips, hops, and paces. As soon as Marie thinks "stop," Cannon sits. Puppy intuition trusts what it cannot see.

Puppies sense your emotions, read your body language, and hear your voice. Their intuition makes the leap between what is and what is not. One afternoon when I walked back to the house after a canine bathroom break with Pip, one of our border collies, I thought, "It's time to do her nails." Instead of heading to our back door, Pip ran to the barn and leapt on my grooming table. Pip knew she was going to be groomed. She ran to the barn and not the house.

Puppies study people. They read between the lines. In the same way you try to predict when your puppy needs to go outside to eliminate, your puppy tries to anticipate what you want. Does a smile on your face mean "Good dog," or "Let's go play ball?" If you slam the door and shout at the kids, does that indicate it's time to hide underneath the table or run up-stairs to an empty bedroom? Does the droop in your shoulders show you are sad and need a puppy to jump on your lap? In the unity of tao, no sep-aration exists between puppy and person. Intuition draws us together and makes us one.

As Logan, my golden retriever, stretches his neck, my fingers rest in his thick golden ruff. He moves closer to me, and I lean into him. We press against each other until I cannot tell where he stops and I begin. Two like souls sitting together watching the sunrise. This morning as I write in my office, I still feel him next to me, a part of me. I see through his eyes and he sees through mine. What I feel is an invisible bond that connects and courses between us. We unite in body and spirit. I ask myself, "Whose eyes?" The answer: "Ours."

Part 2 | The Way of Skillful Living

Chapter 8
Discover the Inner Puppy

Jane hikes the rocky Maine coastline with her flat-coated retriever. Jason watches basketball, baseball, and wrestling on his forty-two-inch wide-screen television while his cattle dog lies at his feet. Molly and Randy's three children play fetch with their Chesapeake Bay retriever in their swimming pool and at the lake.

Before you add a puppy to your life, think about your lifestyle. It's easy to decide if yin or yang predominates in your activities. Review how you spend your spare time. Active yang people hike, bike, play sports, or garden—dynamic activities that involve high energy and movement. Mellow yin people stay home, watch television, crochet, or read books—laidback activities that do not require much physical exertion.

Figure out your favorite interests. Then, choose a puppy who matches your lifestyle. A border collie is bred to run a hundred miles a day and requires extensive running, biking, or walking. However, a shih tzu's idea of action is to move to another person's lap. Decide if you want a family pet, exercise partner, service dog, hunting dog, personal and property protector, or conformation, agility, tracking, herding, fly ball, or obedience show dog. To select a puppy that fits your needs, empty your mind, follow your heart, do your homework, and listen to your intuition.

EMPTY YOUR MIND

Dogs are more than long or short hair; one hundred pounds or twenty-eight pounds; erect or drop ears; brindle, solid, or harlequin colors; and docked or saber tails. Don't get trapped into thinking you can have only a "red" Doberman, a female, or a specific bloodline.

Determine what characteristics you prefer, but don't let preconceived ideas trap you into making the wrong decision. I searched for a breeder for my next golden retriever puppy for six months. Before the litter was due, I informed the breeder that I wanted a girl, I brought home a boy, Logan. In twenty-nine years of living with golden retrievers, Logan is the best of the best. He is the rarest of show dogs—intelligent, enthusiastic, hard working, and happy. He loves life and loves dog shows. If I had insisted that I wanted a girl, I would have missed out on a great show dog and a super friend.

An empty mind allows you to choose freely. Stripped of a list of requirements, you pick the right puppy.

FOLLOW YOUR HEART

You want an eight-week-old, female, Nova Scotia duck-tolling retriever from Maine—but what do you *need*? Inside your heart of hearts, what floats your boat? And I don't mean water. Relationships turn on more than appearances. Surface is not substance. In order to discover the inner puppy, you need to figure out the inner beauty. What defines a good relationship for you? Sara needs a dog that walks where she walks, sleeps where she sleeps, licks her face, and clings to her. Liz likes an independent dog that hangs alone, watches from afar, and stays on the floor when she comes home after work.

When you follow your heart, decide what you want, then determine what you need. Be prepared to dig deep. You think, "But I can love any dog." It's true, but a dog's attitude toward you, how he shows affection, whether he wags his tail, grins, or remains aloof affects your opinion of the relationship. By identifying what you need, you will not feel disappointed, frustrated, overwhelmed, or rejected when a Siberian husky does not get up from the couch when you come home, a standard poodle springs four feet in the air to greet visitors, or a soft-coated wheaten terrier leaps into your cousin's lap and sleeps with her when she spends the night.

When you follow your heart, you know what you need, and nothing else matters.

Do Your Homework

To find a purebred puppy that matches your lifestyle, family, and interests, do your homework. Research the breed, find a responsible breeder, pay attention to the parents, assess the puppy's living conditions, and evaluate the puppy. If you prefer a mixed-breed dog from a shelter or a rescue puppy, you may or may not have access to the breeder, parents, or the puppy's home life, but you can still evaluate the puppy's personality.

Logan matches the characteristics of the breed standard for golden retrievers.

1. Research the breed.

Before selecting a puppy, research the breed. The American Kennel Club (AKC) recognizes 150 breeds. Study the breed standard for the dog you want to investigate. The breed standard describes golden retrievers as "A symmetrical, powerful, active dog." Male goldens stand 23 to 24 inches tall at the withers and weigh 65 to 75 pounds. Female goldens stand between 21½ to 22½ inches tall and weigh between 55 and 65 pounds. Although the breed standard describes golden retrievers as "friendly," it doesn't say they are "in-your-face" friendly dogs. Golden retrievers love to get up close and personal all the time. If you prefer a dog that is not demonstrative, check out a saluki, chow chow, or Shiba Inu.

To learn about a specific breed, talk to people who live with them. Ask them what they enjoy or dislike about the breed. For example, an Afghan's long-haired coat needs to be brushed at least three times a week. If you don't like grooming, do not buy an Old English sheepdog, rough collie, or Maltese. Look for a short-coated, low maintenance breed such as a Labrador retriever, corgi, or pug.

Determine if the breed's exercise requirements fit your lifestyle. Greyhounds, border collies, and vizslas love to run and need daily exercise. If you don't want to spend your spare time running, jogging, or going on long walks, perhaps a bulldog, dachshund, or Japanese Chin will suit your exercise requirements.

Size matters. A male Irish wolfhound that stands 32 inches tall and weighs 120 pounds does not make a good apartment dog. However, a Chinese crested that stands 12 inches tall and weighs 9.5 pounds makes an ideal apartment dweller.

2. Find a responsible breeder.

Breeders who care about the puppies they breed provide appropriate health clearances, offer a written guarantee certifying the dog's health, furnish references, and state they will take the dog back at any time during his life if you cannot keep the dog. Ask the seller for references and the name of the dog's veterinarian. If the seller cannot provide references or the veterinarian's name, do not buy the puppy.

Reliable breeders keep good records. They vaccinate, worm, and feed high-quality food. They wait until a female dog is at least two years old before she's bred. They breed her only once a year. When the dog turns seven years old, she is no longer part of their breeding program.

Responsible breeders have health clearances for the breeding pair. The basic health clearances are: hip (OFA or PennHIP), eye (CERF), and heart (SAS).

Orthopedic Foundation of Animals (OFA)

Veterinarians x-ray hips and elbows to evaluate genetic and orthopedic changes. Then, they submit X-rays to the OFA for evaluation and certification. There are seven evaluation categories: normal (excellent, good, and fair), borderline, and dysplastic (mild, moderate, and severe). OFA preliminary evaluation for hip dysplasia can happen as early as four months. Official certification occurs at twenty-four months.

University of Pennsylvania Hip Improvement Program (PennHIP)

Certified PennHIP veterinarians take three X-rays to measure hip-joint laxity and congruity, and the existence or potential for degenerative joint disorder. The PennHIP procedure can be performed as early as sixteen weeks. However, readings at six or twelve months are more predictive.

Canine Eye Registration Foundation (CERF)

Veterinary ophthalmologists test for genetic eye defects and certify a dog free of heritable eye disease. CERF tests can be performed on 8-week-old puppies. However, some diseases will not appear until later. For example, hereditary cataracts show up between 6 to 8 months. However, progressive retinal atrophy (PRA) can be diagnosed in Irish setters as early as 6 weeks.

Subaortic Stenosis (SAS)

Veterinarians listen to the heart to detect any heart murmurs. However, all heart murmurs do not indicate SAS. If a heart murmur presents, a veterinarian performs additional diagnostic tests to determine if the problem is SAS.

A breeder might have additional health clearances to share with you. Some breeds have genetic predispositions to epilepsy, von Willebrand's disease, cervical vertebral instability (or Wobbler's syndrome), deafness, eye abnormalities, or thyroid disorders.

Responsible breeders answer your questions and teach you about the breed. They interview you. Frequently, they want references about you from your veterinarian. If sellers will ship a dog to you without meeting you or asking you questions, avoid them.

Recognizing good breeders is easy. They breed to improve the breed. Their goal is to produce dogs with excellent conformation, health, soundness, and temperament. They work their dogs and show them. Their adult dogs are well mannered, friendly, and obedient. Puppies are whelped inside. The whelping box and play area are kept clean. The breeder and other family members or helpers play with the puppies and expose them to different noises, sights, sounds, animals, children, and adults.

3. Pay attention to the parents.

Whether you purchase a mixed-breed or a purebred dog, ask to see the parents. Are they friendly, aggressive, shy, or independent? Can you touch them? Do you like them? Pay close attention to the puppy's mother. Can you touch or hold her? Does she bark, whine, or act aggressive?

Puppies learn from their mother. If she is warm, friendly, and nurturing, the puppies will follow her lead. However, if the mother is aggressive, territorial, and aloof, the puppies often develop the same characteristics. Do not buy a puppy if the breeders will not allow you to meet the mother.

Many breeders use another breeder's stud dog. Ask for the stud dog breeder's telephone number so you can call to make an appointment to visit him if the dog lives in your area. If the stud dog's breeder is not local, you can still ask questions about the stud dog during a telephone conversation.

4. **Assess the puppy's living conditions.**

I know an individual who buys dogs with excellent bloodlines for his breeding stock. However, knowledgeable people will not buy his puppies. He breeds too many puppies and keeps them outside in small kennel runs with their mothers. The puppies are exposed to wind, rain, snow, and heat. He never socializes them, gives them toys, or exposes them to other people, animals, or objects. As a result, his eight-week-old puppies are noise-sensitive, people-wary, hyper and/or timid. Never buy a puppy from anyone who will not let you inspect where the puppies and mothers live.

Puppies learn from day one. When you enter a breeder's house, kennel, or yard, look around carefully. Evaluate the environment. Do the puppies have toys? Ask what the breeder has done to expose and socialize the puppies to other people, noises, children, animals, and situations.

Find out if the puppies were whelped inside the house or if they live permanently in an outdoor kennel run. Responsible breeders keep the whelping box and play area clean. If it contains puddles and piles, the puppies do not learn to separate their play space from their elimination area. Puppies that grow up in a dirty environment are harder to house-train.

If you bring home a puppy from a rescue group, ask for the puppy's history. If that is unavailable, ask for input from the foster family. When you purchase a puppy from a shelter or Humane Society, watch and play with the puppy in an outdoor area or indoor room. You will have a better chance of observing the puppy's real personality.

Do not buy a puppy from a pet store. Most pet-store puppies do not come from responsible breeders. Frequently, pet-store dogs have health and behavior problems. I cannot recommend buying a puppy from a pet

A healthy puppy.

store because you cannot see the parents, talk to the breeder, see copies of the parents' health clearances, or inspect the litter's living conditions.

5. Evaluate the puppy.

Assess the puppy's condition and the health of the parents. A puppy's coat should be shiny and thick, without bald spots. The skin should be smooth without scales, crusty areas, or dandruff. Healthy gums are pink. Teeth are white. The puppy's breath should not smell rancid or sour. There should not be any lumps on the puppy's body. The puppy should be sound on all four legs while walking, running, and playing. Check for diarrhea, vomiting, or runny eyes, nose, ears, or anal area. Look for fleas and ticks in a puppy's coat. If a puppy constantly itches, has red, inflamed ears, and discharge from his nose, the puppy may have allergies or other health issues. After you buy the puppy, bring her to your veterinarian for a professional health check.

Watch the puppy interact with his littermates.

To figure out which puppy will suit you and your family, evaluate a litter when they are at least seven weeks old. Before seven weeks, their personalities and physical characteristics are not fully developed. Perform the following exercises during the day when the puppy is normally awake and active. Before a puppy eats is a good time to observe puppy behavior. If possible, bring someone along to help you with the exercises. Remember, if you spend your free time sitting quietly while you cross-stitch and quilt, look for a more mellow, quiet, yin puppy. If you enjoy hiking and jogging, watch for an active, alert, yang puppy. Seven exercises will indicate a puppy's awareness, confidence, adaptability, sensitivity, and inhibitions. By watching, following, raising, separating, holding, touching, and hearing exercises, you will discover the inner puppy.

1. Watching.

Observe how the puppies act and play. Watch to see which puppy initiates play, hides in the corner, bosses other puppies around, eats first, explores the outer reaches, rests quietly, or waits. Puppies with more yang energy push other puppies out of their way. They jump on top of littermates. They hang their head or drape a front leg over another puppy's shoulder area. Yang puppies leap, run, and search for new adventures. They are the first dog to greet you, jump on your legs, run to the door, or bark at you. Brave explorers, they are frequently the first puppy to escape from the whelping box. They lead and expect other puppies to get out of their way. Yang puppies are brave, independent, assertive, inquisitive, happy, cranky, or aloof.

Puppies with more yin energy allow other puppies to displace them from the food bowl, take their toys, and push them away. Gentle souls, they submit instead of assert. Yin puppies can be mellow, shy, happy, curious, excitable, timid, or distant. They play and run, but they spend more time quietly waiting, resting, sleeping, or in retreat from other people and activities.

You do not have to evaluate every puppy. Ask the breeder to remove any puppies you do not want to assess to a separate area. It is easier to observe interactions with fewer puppies.

2. Following.

Take a puppy with you to a different area in the house or yard. Set the puppy on the ground. Move a few steps from the puppy. See if the puppy follows you. Then, skip, run, clap your hands, and call "puppy, puppy, puppy" in a happy voice as you move away. Watch the puppy's behavior.

Yang puppies run after you, nip at your heels, seek you out, or ignore you and explore other areas. Yin puppies remain rooted to the spot, run and hide under a chair or behind a bush, or slowly follow you. Yin puppies overwhelm easily. They need your encouragement and support, but in a different way. Running, skipping, and clapping your hands might be too loud and energetic. Frequently, yin puppies follow better if you whistle. Turn away. Do not stare at them, crouch down, and run your fingers through the grass. Whistle. Call happily, "puppy, puppy, puppy." Observe the puppy's reaction.

Lift up and hold a puppy in your arms.

3. Raising.

Lift up the puppy and hold her in your arms. Yang puppies look around, lick your face, or struggle in your arms. Yin puppies hide their head under your elbow, pant, panic, freeze, or lick their lips.

4. Separating.

Remove a puppy from his littermates to a different area. Close the door. Yang puppies act. They bark, scratch the door, or explore the new area. Yin puppies freeze or fly. They whimper, bark, cower in silence against the door, or hide in the new area. Next, sit near the puppy with a toy in your hand. Can you get the puppy interested in the toy? Play "toy" with the puppy. Now, take the toy away from the puppy. Watch the puppy's reaction. Yang puppies refuse to release a toy, chase, growl, lunge, or snap at you. Yin puppies accept, yield, and forget about the toy.

5. Holding.

Sit down. Hold a puppy in your lap for three minutes. Yang puppies struggle until you release them. Or, they struggle for thirty to

A yang puppy doesn't mind being separated from his littermates.

Hold a puppy in your lap.

ninety-five seconds, and then relax. Yin puppies submit immediately. Or, they resist, then quickly calm down.

6. Touching.

Sit on the ground with a puppy. Touch the puppy on his head. Rub his ears. Hold each paw in your hand. Run your hands along his body,

Touch the puppy everywhere.

inside his back legs, and down his tail. Pass your fingers along his gums inside his mouth. Yang puppies often resist or fight your efforts. Yin puppies accept and allow your touch.

7. Hearing.

Ask a friend to drop a book on the floor while he stands at least eight feet behind the puppy. Does the puppy respond with a look or glance? Does the puppy run away or toward the book? Next, drop a metal bowl on the floor. Does a harsher sound change how the puppy responds? Yang puppies might startle, but then they inspect. Yin puppies react and retreat.

LISTEN TO YOUR INTUITION

You followed your heart, researched the breed, met the breeders, inspected litters, visited shelters, evaluated the puppies, and emptied your mind, but now you need to make a decision. Bring your awareness to each puppy. Pause. Relax. In silence, intuition grows. Allow the subtle knowing of tao to enter your mind. In peaceful, quiet certainty, choose. When you act from inner wisdom, you know the puppy to select, understand why, and do not have any doubts.

Chapter 9
First Days

Tao gives life to all beings.
Nature nourishes them.
Fellow creatures shape them.
Circumstances complete them.[12]

Elizabeth found the perfect cocker spaniel breeder two hours from her house. The puppies were eight weeks old and ready to meet their new families. Elizabeth asked her sister Ann to drive with her to the small town. At 8:00 A.M. on Saturday, they started driving. By 10:15 they had found the country lane and white farmhouse that Beverly, the cocker spaniel breeder, had described on the telephone.

Eight, wiggling, happy cockers greeted them when they walked into Beverly's garage. Two hours later Elizabeth had made her selection and was ready to drive home. However, Elizabeth had forgotten to plan for the puppy's journey home. She had not brought a crate, box, blanket, collar, or leash to keep the puppy safe and comfortable on the drive to her house. Elizabeth forgot to bring toys, treats, water bowl, or poop bags. Luckily, the puppy came with a small collar. Beverly gave them a cardboard box with layers of newspapers for a crate, food, bowl, leash, and plastic bags for the drive home.

A two-hour car ride, six-hour plane trip with one layover, or thirty-minute outing require different amounts of preparation to bring a puppy home safely and comfortably. Whether your trip will be long or short, you

still need to plan ahead, bring appropriate puppy traveling gear and supplies, and ask for someone to help you. Ask your husband, best friend, or
cousin to come with you when you pick up the puppy. A second person
can hold the puppy and watch the luggage while you exchange airline tick-
ets and a health certificate for boarding passes at the ticket counter. Another pair of eyes can watch the puppy while you drive.

If you must stay overnight before bringing the puppy home, make
reservations at a motel that accepts dogs. Remember, you cannot leave a
puppy in the motel room while you go out to eat. Choose a motel with
room service or restaurants that deliver. Or, take your puppy with you and
order at a fast food drive-in window and eat in your car or motel room.

Before you travel with a puppy, limit his intake of solid food. When
you fly, do not give the puppy solid food for at least four hours before
your flight. When you drive, ask the breeder to not feed the puppy any
solid food for at least two hours before your trip.

During the trip, do not sedate the dog. Instead, give your puppy Rescue
Remedy, a flower essence remedy that relieves stress in animals and people.
Rescue Remedy does not drug or tranquilize puppies, yet it calms them.

During a car ride, strap down a hard plastic kennel in your backseat.
If you have an SUV or sport wagon, flip down the seats and strap, tie, or
bungee cord a crate in place. In the car, store treats, toys, water bowl,
water, paper towels, and plastic bags in a lidded storage container.

Contact the airline to learn its rules and regulations. Follow them. For
example, airlines do not allow puppies in exit rows. Whenever possible,
schedule a nonstop flight. Try to avoid flying during peak hours. Plan extra
time at the airport to check in with your puppy. Reservation agents will inspect the puppy's health certificate. Ask your breeder to have the puppy's
health certificate prepared when you pick up the dog.

Puppies fly in cargo or under your seat when you are a passenger. Not
all airlines fly puppies. If an airline permits dogs, you must reserve a space
for them in advance because airlines limit the number of puppies that can
travel inside a plane at the same time. Airlines that ship dogs in cargo have

Puppy in a carry-on bag.

specific requirements concerning age, kennels, crate identification, food, water, and weather. For example, airlines in Phoenix refuse to ship puppies during the summer because of the heat.

When I fly with a puppy, I use a soft-sided, open, mesh carrier with a fleecy liner that fits under the airplane seat. The zippered openings allow me to reach in and pet the puppy without the puppy ever leaving the carrier. In the carrier pockets I store treats, toys, collapsible water bowl, water, paper towels, and plastic bags.

SAFETY-PROOF YOUR HOUSE
BEFORE THE PUPPY ARRIVES

Puppies explore the world with their mouths. They live by the motto, "If I can find it, I can eat it." Puppies chew everything. Move your glasses

Safety-proof your house!

to a safe place. Store your coins, paper clips, pens, TV remote, socks, and candles in an area out of puppy reach. Puppies love children's stuffed toys, action figures, games, crayons, markers, and puzzle pieces. Teach your children to pick up their toys, and close their closet and bedroom doors. Safety-proof your house, swimming pool, and yard *before* the puppy comes home. Electrical dangers, poisons, plants, children's toys, and household objects can hurt, seriously injure, or threaten the life of your puppy. Puppy-proof to prevent serious injury to active, curious, and chewing puppies.

If you suspect your puppy has ingested a toxic plant, chemical solution, or drug; been shocked; submerged under water in the pool; or bitten by a scorpion, spider, or snake, contact your veterinarian immediately. The telephone number for the ASPCA Animal Poison Control Center is

1–888–426–4435. The center operates 24 hours a day, 7 days a week, 365 days a year, and charges $50 per case.

ELECTRICAL HAZARDS

One hundred twenty volts of electricity flow through outlets, electrical cords, and extension cords to appliances such as hair dryers, televisions, stereos, lights, computers, irons, and alarm clocks. Install electrical outlet covers; remove extension cords; and bundle, cover, and hide electrical cords. If you cannot remove items or objects, spray them with Bitter Apple or coat objects with Listerine on a regular basis. Watch your puppy at all times. Then, you can avoid accidents and injuries.

POISONS

Poisons lurk in bathroom cabinets, kitchen cupboards, garages, and storage units. Bathroom cabinets contain prescription medications, rubbing alcohol, fingernail polish remover, diet pills, cold medicines, antidepressants, aspirin, acetaminophen, ibuprofen, deodorants, shampoo, and conditioner—all potentially lethal items for puppies.

Kitchen cupboards hold toxic bleach, ammonia, cleanser, soap, ant bait, mice bait, insect sprays, furniture polish, and liquid potpourri. Tobacco, nicotine patches and gum, and moldy garbage can poison dogs. Avoid feeding puppies the following foods: avocados, chocolate, coffee, grapes, macadamia nuts, raisins, onions, or any beer, liquor, or wine.

Garages and storage units store deadly antifreeze, non-water-based paint, gasoline, kerosene, lamp oil, turpentine, fertilizer, and weed killer.

To keep your puppy safe, install child-proof locks on cupboards and cabinets. Lock storage units. Buy wastepaper baskets and garbage containers with lids that can be tightly secured. If you cannot lock a cupboard, move toxic items to a higher shelf or put them in a place the puppy cannot reach. Always watch a puppy during his wanderings.

DANGEROUS PLANTS

A plant's appearance is deceptive. Although they look green, leafy, and lush, many plants are toxic to dogs. If you are not sure if your plants are "puppy-safe," check with your veterinarian, library, horticultural center, or county extension agent. They can help you determine the safety of your plants, trees, shrubs, and bushes. Indoor and outdoor plants can be toxic for dogs. The following list contains a variety of toxic indoor and outdoor plants.

Toxic Indoor Plants

Aloe vera, baby's breath, corn plant, croton, dieffenbachia, Easter lily, eucalyptus, ficus, ivy, jade, mistletoe berries, pothos, Norfolk island pine, philodendrons, rubber plant, schefflera, and snake plant.

Toxic Outdoor Plants

Asparagus fern, azalea, bird of paradise, cactus, chrysanthemum, foxglove, geranium, hydrangea, lantana, lily of the valley, jimsonweed, morning glory, nightshade, oleander, rhubarb, tomato plant, wild mushrooms, wisteria, daffodil, jonquil, and tulip bulbs.

SWIMMING POOLS, HOT TUBS, AND PONDS

Water lures puppies like warm chocolate brownies attract children. Fences are not enough. Small puppy bodies can wiggle through four- or six-inch-wide wrought iron openings. Determined puppy paws can burrow under cyclone fences. Busy noses and mouths chew and lift hot tub covers

An exercise pen.

or explore the pond. To prevent accidents, drowning, and poisoning, fasten a tight wire-mesh screen against a fence and underneath it. Lock the gate, store cleaning supplies, and install locks on the hot tub cover. Clean the blue-green algae out of the pond so a puppy won't ingest it and get sick. Teach an older puppy how to swim and safely leave a pool. Swimming is more than paddling in circles or fetching a ball. Dogs must learn how to exit from a pool.

There are times when you cannot watch a puppy. All dogs need shelter and a safe place to stay when you cannot supervise them. Dog crates, exercise pens, and kennel runs keep puppies safe and protected. They are *temporary* housing solutions. Puppies should not be kept isolated in crates, pens, and runs for more than two hours during the day. At night, puppies can stay in crates longer because they are sleeping and their metabolic system slows down.

Exercise or "x-" pens are made out of sturdy wire-mesh panels that unfold to create a fenced-in space. Exercise pens range in height from

Chain-link kennel runs.

A hard-sided vinyl crate.

A soft-sided crate.

twenty-four to forty-eight inches. You can attach a wire-mesh panel to enclose the top completely. Two x-pens can be combined to create a puppy play area.

Kennel runs consist of chain-link fencing or welded-rod mesh panels. They can be any size or length. A kennel run can be ten by twenty feet or ten by six feet; it's your choice. Standard panel sizes are three by four feet, five by five feet, and other custom sizes.

Dog kennels can be soft-sided carriers with zippered openings; hard molded plastic with side vents, metal grate door, and spring-loaded latches; or wire mesh with fasteners. What you choose depends on whether you are using a kennel for traveling or for home use. When I bring a puppy on a plane, the carrier must fit under the seat. A soft-sided mesh carrier works perfectly. When I drive with a puppy, I use a hard plastic kennel that seatbelts hold securely in place. At home I use a combination of hard molded plastic, metal mesh kennels, and exercise pens. In the bedroom I use an exercise pen. In other areas of the house, I place dog crates or exercise pens. The puppy "house" I choose depends on the space, light, heat,

A baby-gate contains a puppy in the kitchen.

and traffic pattern in a particular room. All my crates for home use are large enough so a puppy can stand, sit, lie down, and turn around. The crate and exercise pen contain toys and a dog bed. In addition, the exercise pen also contains a litter box.

Baby-gates contain puppies in a particular room or prevent a dog's access to a dining room, kitchen, bathroom, or bedroom. Place them at the top or bottom of stairs. To work as a barricade, baby-gates must be securely fastened. Check that the baby-gate does not contain openings that are wide enough to allow a small puppy to squeeze through or a large puppy to trap his head.

Small Necessities

Four items smooth the transition from the breeder's house to your home: bowls, treats, toys, and odor neutralizers or enzymatic cleaners. Chapter 12 describes appropriate training and grooming materials for puppies.

1. Bowls.

Buy two bowls. I prefer stainless steel or ceramic. Use one bowl for water and the other bowl for food. Clean them on a regular basis.

2. Treats.

Dog treats range from carrots to ice cubes to doggy biscuits. Find a small treat your puppy likes. You will use it as a reward during puppy schooling sessions.

3. Toys.

Puppies like to gnaw on hard surfaces such as marrow bones and Kongs. Kongs are natural rubber, flexible, bulbous, cone-shaped toys that have small and large openings on either end where dog biscuits, kibble, a teaspoon of peanut butter, or a slice of apple or carrot can be stuffed.

A large puppy needs a big toy.

Puppies that are cutting teeth and have sore gums enjoy chewing on a wet washcloth that has been frozen in the freezer or a Kong that has been frozen with chicken broth, rice, or canned dog food inside it.

Select dog toys carefully: choose the right size and type for your puppy. A toy that is too small can be swallowed. Do not buy toys with plastic eyes or parts that can be torn off and swallowed. If a puppy tears apart a soft toy, remove it. This prevents the dog from eating the plastic squeaker or stuffing inside it.

If you play with a ball, roll the ball on the ground. Do not toss the ball high in the air so the puppy leaps up to grab it. Wait to teach your puppy to catch a Frisbee until after he is a year old. Puppies that jump high and twist can physically injure themselves.

4. Odor neutralizer or enzymatic cleaner.

If a puppy defecates inside the house, pick it up by placing your hand inside a plastic bag to remove it. Once the pile is safely inside the bag, remove your hand and raise the plastic sides. Now, you can easily bring it to the garbage. Return to the area and clean it with an odor neutralizer or enzymatic cleaner that you can buy at a pet store or from a dog catalog. Buy a pooper scooper to pick up piles in your yard.

If a puppy urinates on the floor, place paper towels over the area. Next, place newspaper on top of the paper towels. Then, step on top of the papers. Remove the papers and repeat with new ones until there is no longer a wet spot. Then, clean the area with an odor neutralizer or enzymatic cleaner. Water is not enough to eliminate scent from your carpet and floors.

Nighttime Essentials

The first night is as important as the first day. The first night, I sleep with the new puppy. No, I don't crawl into the exercise pen or kennel. I bring out an air mattress, cover it with sheets and blankets, and sleep on the floor with the puppy. When Red Sun Rising, a 10-month-old golden retriever rescue dog, came home with me from the shelter, we spent the first night in my office. I rested on the couch while Red slept on the floor, my hand curled in his fur.

Leaving littermates, a foster home, or the shelter for a new house disturbs most dogs. Turn your welcome mat into a floor pillow, mattress, or couch. Show the puppy you care by spending the first night with him. Allow your heartbeat and the rhythm of your breathing to ease his entry into your life. By the second night, the puppy is ready to sleep in an exercise pen or crate in your bedroom. After one week passes, the puppy easily accepts new routines of eating, house-training, snuggling, and playing. Ease the puppy's transition to your home. Spend time and stick close. You won't regret it. If you ignore the beginning, you will never reach the end.

Chapter 10
Tao of Diet

Jim and Calhoun, an eight-month-old basset hound, play "bassetball" and go on camping trips in the mountains. Jim takes Calhoun with him to the hardware store, bank, and Burger King. When Jim drives, he opens the truck windows, and they listen to Elvis Presley belt out "You Ain't Nothing but a Hound Dog." Jim wants the best for Calhoun, and that includes his diet. Before he brought Calhoun home, Jim researched the breed. He learned that Calhoun's ancestors were French scent hounds. They were bred to trail rabbits and bay while they track. Basset hounds are short dogs. They stand between thirteen and fifteen inches at the withers, but their long, strong bodies weigh between forty and fifty-five pounds. To prevent Calhoun from getting fat, a common basset hound problem, Jim carefully planned Calhoun's diet.

Basset hounds, Chihuahuas, Labrador retrievers, and Great Danes have breed-specific feeding requirements. As an adult, a Chihuahua weighs between two and six pounds. A Great Dane weighs between 120 and 170 pounds. A Labrador hunting dog who lives outside in a kennel run in Minneapolis, Minnesota, needs more calories than a Labrador who lives inside as a family pet in Miami, Florida. To meet the nutritional needs of tiny (teacup or toy), small, medium, large, and giant puppies, the tao of diet follows three guidelines: simple, adaptable, and natural.

A simple diet recognizes that puppies need foods that contain easily assimilated protein, carbohydrates, fats, minerals, and vitamins. Protein develops, repairs, and replaces muscle. Carbohydrates add energy. Fats provide fatty acids, which promote a healthy skin and coat. Minerals and vitamins aid in the formation of bones and promote the function of nerves, muscles, blood, and fluids.

An adaptable diet accepts that puppy, adolescent, adult, and senior dogs have different nutritional requirements. It acknowledges that age, weather, geographic location, amount of exercise, activity, and breed affect the type and amount of food a dog needs. The diet adjusts and evolves as the puppy matures.

A natural diet follows a taoist path. You realize that to raise healthy puppies, dogs need high-quality food and fresh filtered water. Depending on the diet you feed, you wash produce to avoid pesticide contamination, cook meats, feed a variety of foods, and change dog kibble brands at least once a year. A natural diet does not complicate your life. It can be as easy as recognizing the difference between large puppy and small puppy dry food, and feeding the appropriate size kibble for your dog.

Natural diets include the type of food that dogs ate where they originated. Puppies are not fed pizza and potato chips, but balanced, healthy, whole food. To design the best feeding program for a puppy, research the history of the breed, determine the puppy's activity level, review the amount of daily exercise, evaluate the weather, and recognize that as puppies mature, they have different nutritional requirements. Talk to your veterinarian, breeder, and a canine nutrition specialist, and then implement a feeding program that meets the puppy's needs and your lifestyle. Be prepared to modify, improve, and alter the diet as the dog grows.

A correct feeding program produces a puppy with a thin layer of muscle and fat covering his ribs. The puppy's weight fits his age, height, and breed. He does not lose or gain inappropriate amounts of weight. The puppy's waist is tucked, but not drawn up or tight. His coat appears shiny and lush. His skin looks elastic and smooth. He does not have excessive gas. The puppy enjoys eating his food.

Used properly, food energizes a puppy and builds bones and muscles. The puppy should not grow too fast or too slow. To learn the expected rate of growth for your puppy, research the breed, talk to the breeder, find other people who have the same breed, and ask your veterinarian. Closely observe the puppy's weight. If the puppy loses the definition of her ribs and her "lean" look, decrease the amount of food you are feeding. If a puppy appears hungry, licks his bowl, and scavenges for food, increase the quality of dog food ingredients and/or add another meal to your feeding schedule. If you are following feeding guidelines suggested by your veterinarian, breeder, or dog food manufacturer, make an appointment with your veterinarian so the puppy can be checked for worms, parasites, or other health problems that could affect his ability to digest food.

FEEDING SCHEDULE

The easiest way to establish good eating habits is to feed a puppy at the same time every day. If the puppy wanders off before the bowl is empty, wait ten minutes. Then pick up the food dish. Most puppies need to eat four times a day, approximately every four hours from the time they wake, until the time they sleep. However, tiny or extremely young puppies need to eat more often. A "teacup" Yorkshire terrier weighs fewer than four pounds as an adult. A teacup Yorkie puppy does not have the same ability to store fat as a large dog. Depending on the individual, a teacup puppy needs to eat every two to four hours.

However, large and giant puppies have other requirements. A Great Dane puppy weighs 1 to 2 pounds at birth. By sixteen weeks, Great Dane puppies weigh between 50 and 65 pounds. At nine months, they weigh between 85 and 120 pounds. An adult male Great Dane weighs between 120 and 170 pounds. Large and giant breed puppies require food that will not accelerate their growth, but provide slow, even development of bones and joints. Breeders of "big dogs" do not recommend feeding regular puppy food because they believe it boosts growth too quickly. Instead, they recommend feeding specific large and giant puppy food, or premium adult food, or a combination of large and giant puppy food and adult food.

Start by feeding your puppy the same food he ate at his previous home. Give the puppy two weeks to settle in before you make any changes to his diet. During the two weeks, observe the size and quality of his feces and frequency of bowel movements. With careful observation you can determine how easily your puppy assimilates his food.

The type of stool and frequency of bowel movements indicates a puppy's ability to digest food. Firm, small, low-volume stools with fewer bathroom visits indicate high food digestibility. Keep the puppy on the same food if the puppy's hair coat shines and his skin stays smooth, elastic, and pliable. However, if the puppy's skin appears scaly or rough and his hair coat looks dull, carefully inspect his stools. Soft, plentiful stools with frequent bathroom visits suggest low digestibility. Giving a puppy more of the same food will not increase the puppy's ability to digest it. The puppy needs a different dog food that is easier for his body to absorb.

HOW TO CHOOSE THE RIGHT DOG FOOD FOR YOUR PUPPY

What a puppy eats depends on you. Dogs eat home-cooked meals; dry kibble; canned, semi-moist, and raw food; or a combination of dry, canned, and home-cooked. Everyone has her own ideas about what is best. This is what I know. One recipe cannot fit all dogs. It does not matter what your mother, brother, or partner thinks. In order to determine what to feed a puppy, analyze the puppy's activity level, research the breed history, and evaluate your lifestyle. Then, make your decision whether you will feed home-cooked meals, dry food, semi-moist, canned, raw food, or a combination of them.

Home-cooked meals offer an excellent option if you are particular about the ingredients your puppy eats. You select and prepare all the food. However, home-cooked meals require a significant amount of research and time to find the appropriate recipes for your dog. Unfortunately, home-cooked meals do not fit my lifestyle. My solution is to feed our dogs a premium, high-quality, human-grade, meat-based dog food that contains chelated minerals. I prefer meat instead of soy because meat contains more amino acids than soy beans. Depending on my meals, their dog bowls might contain eggs, broccoli, asparagus, mushrooms, spinach, or chicken in addition to the kibble. I insist that any food my dogs eat is preserved naturally without artificial colorings, flavors, or preservatives such as BHT (butylated hydroxytoluene), BHA (butylated hydroxyanisole), or ethoxyquin. BHT, BHA, and ethoxyquin are chemical additives used as preservatives. According to some studies and veterinarians, BHT, BHA, and ethoxyquin can cause serious health problems in dogs.

If you love to spend time in the kitchen, home-cooked meals might suit you perfectly. If that's the case, study canine nutritional guidelines. Know your breed. Calcium over-supplementation causes zinc deficiency in Doberman pinschers. Zinc deficiency leads to skin problems or retards a puppy's growth. West Highland white terriers have a genetic trait that affects the liver's ability to process copper. Westies need a diet low in copper. Home cooking requires that you learn about your breed and a dog's nutritional requirements.

If you feed dry kibble, search for a dog food with different formulas for puppies and adult dogs. Look for the AAFCO (Association of American Feed Control) seal of approval on the dog food. The AAFCO seal indicates that the food has been prepared according to a fixed recipe. A fixed recipe means that the manufacturers always use the same meat. No substitute meats are allowed. The AAFCO seal of approval also indicates that the manufacturer has tested and evaluated the dog food.

Generic dog foods frequently use a variable recipe. With a variable recipe, manufacturers switch ingredients. The protein may be feathers, hair, beaks, or other non-digestible food. Generic dog foods contain lower-quality food and are often mineral deficient. Variable recipes also create situations where the "same" dog food may not agree with a puppy's digestion system. One time, beef products may be used as protein; another time, chicken products are substituted. This causes problems if a puppy can eat chicken, but beef upsets his system.

Be proactive. Learn what your dog needs to maintain good health. Use nutritional resources wisely. Read the label. Contact the dog food manufacturer concerning digestibility and ingredients. Ask if it uses a fixed or variable recipe. If you feed dry dog food, buy a premium, high-quality brand.

The softer texture of canned or semi-moist food either soothes sore puppy gums or does not provide enough crunch for teething puppies. Canned dog food contains a high water content that ranges from 74 to 78 percent. Premium canned dog food contains a higher proportion of meat than low-quality dog food. Canned dog foods often contain soy that appears to look like meat. If you feed canned dog food, buy a premium, high-quality brand. Semi-moist food has a high sugar content. Consistent high sugar intake can stress a dog's pancreas and adrenals. Avoid it.

If you decide to feed raw meat, be careful. Salmonella, parasites, and E. coli are potential problems with uncooked meat. Other issues to watch for are choking or obstructions with bones.

WATER

All dogs need fresh water, and lots of it. Filtered spring water is free of chemicals or impurities that can affect your puppy's health.

HOW TO CHOOSE THE RIGHT TIME
TO SWITCH TO ADULT FOOD

Track the puppy's height, weight, and age. When puppies reach approximately 90 percent of their height and 85 percent of their adult weight, change to an adult food formula. If you have a mixed-breed puppy, ask your veterinarian for advice about when to switch to adult food.

The exact age that a puppy changes to adult food depends on the individual puppy, the breed, and the puppy's activity level. The following chart provides *approximate* age guidelines.

Plan on taking nine days to switch your puppy from puppy food to adult food. However, any time you change foods, use this simple formula to blend the two foods together. Start by mixing ¼ adult food with ¾ puppy food. Use this mixture for at least three days. Next, mix ½ adult food with ½ puppy food. Use this mixture for at least three days. Then, mix ¾ adult food with ¼ puppy food. Use this mixture for at least three days. Finally, serve the adult food without any puppy food mixed into it.

When to Switch to Adult Food

Size	Age
Tiny (Teacup and Toy): up to 15 pounds	8 to 11 months
Small: 15.1 to 25 pounds	8 to 11 months
Medium: 25.1 to 50 pounds	12 months
Large:* 50.1 to 99 pounds	13 to 15 months
Giant:* 99.1+ pounds	14 to 18 months

* Check with your breeder and veterinarian. Many people do not feed regular puppy food because they believe it accelerates growth and causes bone problems in giant and large dogs.

Chapter 11
Good Health Naturally

Logan, our golden retriever puppy, weighed 20.4 pounds at ten weeks. However, Logan's weight did not stop my husband, Jeff, from carrying Logan in his arms for his first visit to the veterinarian's office. Holding Logan prevented him from touching noses with sick dogs and walking on floors that might be contaminated. Jeff carried Logan on each subsequent visit to the veterinarian until Logan completed his series of puppy shots. Although Logan weighed 49.7 pounds at his final visit, carrying him was much easier than treating a sick puppy.

Jeff carries Logan when he weighs 49 pounds.

Four years later, Jeff carries Logan for fun.

Puppies are exposed to disease through contact with another dog's saliva, urine, feces, vomit, or discharge from eyes or nose. Your hands, clothes, and shoes; children's in-line skates and bicycles; and even car tires are potential disease carriers. Highly contagious diseases spread through the air and live in the soil. Normally, a mother's milk, or colostrum, provides temporary protection against disease between six to twenty weeks. However, immunity to disease depends on the mother's health and the physical vitality of each puppy. Mothers can also pass diseases to their puppies.

Protect your puppy by thinking ahead. Place the puppy in a crate and carry her to your veterinarian's office. To prevent a puppy from being exposed to contagious diseases at home, remove your shoes before you enter the house. Ask children to leave in-line skates and skateboards in the garage. Before anyone touches the puppy, wash hands with soap and water. Ask visitors to take off their shoes. If removing shoes is not an option, a solution of one ounce chlorine bleach per quart of water sprayed on shoes destroys most disease-causing organisms. Finally, do not board your puppy at a kennel or bring him to the groomer until his vaccinations are completed. However, do not isolate your puppy from people and other dogs. Chapter 22 explains ways to safely socialize your puppy so that he learns to be friendly with adults, children, and dogs.

People who follow tao recognize that to keep a puppy in optimum health requires specialized veterinary care. Make an appointment for a veterinarian to inspect your puppy. Don't wait. Before forty-eight hours pass, your new puppy should be examined by a veterinarian to determine if the puppy has any health issues. Do not assume you can tell the condition of a puppy by looking at him. Instead, take the puppy to a veterinarian. At the puppy's first visit the veterinarian will examine the dog. She will check the puppy's heartbeat, breathing, temperature, skin and coat condition, mouth, ears, eyes, bones, muscles, lymph nodes, and genitals for congenital or inherited defects such as missing teeth, deafness, or collie eye. Be prepared to give the veterinarian the puppy's history, a list of previous vaccinations and medications, current food, and a fecal sample so it can be tested for worms. If the puppy has serious problems, you can return the puppy to the breeder or shelter. Or, the veterinarian can help you decide the best way to solve the health issue.

FOUR WAYS TO CREATE STRESS-FREE VISITS TO A VETERINARIAN

1. After the initial exam, bring the puppy for a short friendly visit to the veterinarian's office before a puppy's "official" appointment. Take along some treats. Ask the veterinary receptionist, technician, and veterinarian to give the puppy a treat. You want the puppy to learn that a veterinarian's office is a nice place to visit. The number of trips you plan depends on your puppy's attitude. A shy or fearful puppy needs more friendly visits than a confident, bold puppy.

2. After the initial visit, teach a puppy to "sit," "down," and "stay." Puppies that wiggle, squirm, and bounce are difficult to examine. However, if you teach a puppy to sit, lie down, and stay, a veterinarian can easily examine your dog. Chapter 20 explains how to teach "sit," "down," and "stay."

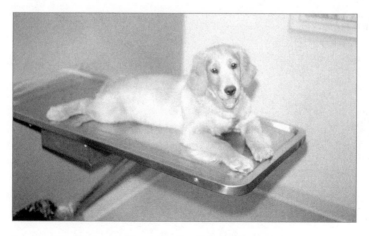

Logan lies down on the examination table.

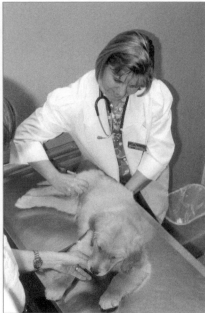

Dr. Christine Stevenson examines Logan.

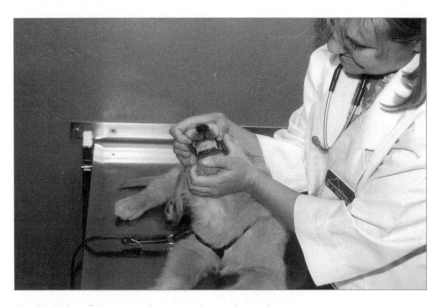

Dr. Christine Stevenson inspects Logan's teeth.

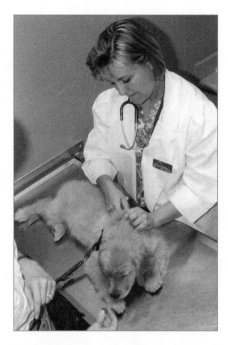

Dr. Christine Stevenson gives Logan a shot.

3. Practice touching the puppy everywhere on her body—ears, stomach, paws, inside her mouth, and between her legs. At home, lightly hold your puppy's paws for ten seconds. Lift her tail. Raise her ears and pretend to look inside. Open her mouth. Rub her belly. Veterinarians and their assistants must touch and hold a puppy to take her temperature, inspect her body, draw blood, or give a shot. Puppies that are accustomed to people touching them anywhere are not scared when a veterinary technician takes their temperature.

4. Bring a puppy's favorite toy and food treats to an appointment. Associate good things with a veterinary exam.

When you take a puppy to see the veterinarian, bring along some small pieces of chicken, cheese, or freeze-dried liver treats, or a special toy or ball. Then, if the puppy becomes uneasy or afraid during an

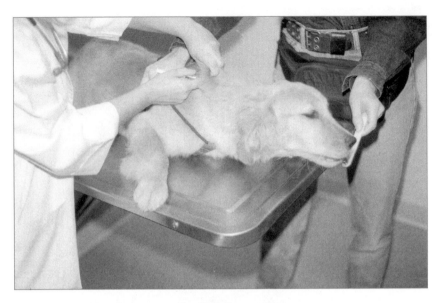

Logan's attention focuses on food during a shot.

exam, give the puppy a piece of chicken while the veterinarian lifts his tail, looks in his ears, or gives him a shot. This reduces the puppy's discomfort. The puppy learns that when a veterinarian or veterinary technician touches him, something pleasant happens *at the same time.* He eats something tasty, or his favorite toy suddenly appears. The puppy learns that good things happen during an exam.

Puppies need vaccinations to protect them against highly contagious diseases. Learn the diseases that are prevalent in your area. The common core dog vaccinations are: distemper virus, parvovirus, hepatitis (adenovirus 2) virus, and rabies virus. However, infectious diseases vary according to region. Work with your veterinarian to determine a vaccination program that works with your dog's health needs and assesses risk factors.

The vaccination protocol I follow was developed by Dr. W. Jean Dodds, a veterinarian who researches and studies the effects that shots using a modified live virus or killed virus have on immunity and health. It uses single-shot vaccinations. Appropriate single-shot vaccinations do not overwhelm a puppy's system if he is in good health. According to Dr. Dodds:

> "Current recommendations for vaccinating dogs have changed significantly in response to increasing evidence and concerns about the need for and safety of routinely giving annual booster vaccines. The new protocols include: 1) giving puppies the designated "core" vaccines followed by a booster at one year of age; 2) administering further boosters in a combination vaccine every three years, or as split components alternating every other year until; 3) the dog reaches geriatric age. At which time booster vaccination is usually unnecessary and may be unadvisable. In the intervening years and in the case of geriatric dogs, circulating immunity can be evaluated by measuring serum vaccine antibody titers as an indication of the presence of 'immune memory.' Antibody titers [are] an alternative to dog owners who prefer not to follow the conventional practice of giving boosters. Reliable serologic vaccine titering is available from several university and commercial laboratories and the cost is reasonable."

A veterinarian draws blood so it can be sent to a laboratory that performs tests to determine a dog's probable immunity to the distemper virus and parvovirus. A titer is the result of a blood test that indicates whether a dog has immunity to a specific viral infection. A high titer indicates the dog does not need re-vaccination at this time. A low titer indicates a lack of protection and the need for a booster vaccine.

Three weeks after a dog receives a shot to raise a low titer, ask the veterinarian to draw another titer. If the titer does not indicate better

Puppy Vaccination Schedule

6 to 7 weeks	Distemper (Galaxy-D) or Distemper-Measles (Vanguard DM)
8 to 9 weeks	Parvovirus, killed
11 to 12 weeks	Parvovirus, killed
12 to 14 weeks	Distemper (Galaxy-D, not Vanguard DM)
16 to 18 weeks	Distemper (Galaxy-D, not Vanguard DM)*
16 to 20 weeks	Parvovirus, killed*
24 weeks	Rabies
12 months	Single booster shot parvo and distemper given three weeks apart. Three weeks later, give rabies killed three-year vaccine.

* Separate distemper 7 to 10 days from parvo booster.

protection, it means the dog is a non-responder to the titer test. If the dog is a non-responder to a titer test, follow the three-year vaccination cycle and administer the appropriate booster.

Puppies can experience harmful vaccination reactions, varying from mild to severe. Some breeds such as miniature schnauzers, Great Danes, Weimaraners, and Akitas are more sensitive to vaccinations than other breeds. However, any puppy can be susceptible. After a single, five-in-one, or seven-in-one vaccination (a shot where five or seven vaccines are combined in one shot), puppies might lose their appetite, itch, shake their head, and experience facial swelling or hives. Occasionally, anaphylactic shock—a severe allergic reaction to a vaccine—occurs. Then, breathing

Alternative Puppy Vaccination Protocol

The following protocol minimizes the number of vaccine antigens.

9 to 10 weeks	MLV distemper and parvovirus (Intervet Progard Puppy DPV)
14 weeks	MLV distemper and parvovirus (Intervet Progard Puppy DPV)
24 weeks	Rabies
12 months	Distemper and Parvovirus MLV (Intervet Progard Puppy DPV) Three weeks later give rabies killed three-year vaccine.

Note: According to Dr. Dodds, the only minimum antigen option for hepatitis vaccine (adenovirus 2) is Pfizer's Vangard distemper + adenovirus 2. Consult your veterinarian about it.

problems, vomiting, diarrhea, seizures, collapse, and sometimes death result. Severe reactions usually happen right away. Moderate and mild responses happen after you arrive home, later that evening, or during the next day.

Safeguard your puppy's well-being by waiting in the veterinarian's reception area for thirty minutes before driving home. After you arrive home, stay home. Do not leave the puppy. If the puppy should experience a reaction, contact your veterinarian immediately.

The timing of shots also plays a role in a puppy's physical reaction to a vaccine injection. Do not wait to vaccinate your puppy until the day before you leave her at a boarding kennel or take her with you on a trip. Plan for the puppy to receive any shot at least three weeks in advance of major changes or potential stresses, such as a move to a new house, the birth of a child, or a change in employment. If the puppy is ill or has an infection, do not vaccinate her. Wait until the puppy is healthy and your professional and personal life is steady.

The puppy's well-being depends on you. Your responsibility is to provide proactive health care and appropriate veterinary care. With your help, your puppy will be fit for life.

Chapter 12
You Can't Drink Water with a Fork

Jaylin walks barefoot on the narrow strip of sand where the ocean meets the land with Fyre, her six-month-old Dalmatian. She drapes the leash over her right shoulder, leaving her hands free. Fyre leaps over broken driftwood and dodges the remains from yesterday's storm. The rolling surf catches the imprints left by their feet and scrubs the sandy beach clean. Twenty breezy minutes pass.

Jaylin spots a rangy large dog running free in the distance. Fyre sees the dog and charges in his direction. The leash slips from Jaylin's shoulder and falls to the ground. Jaylin dives and catches the leash in her hands. She holds tight, but Fyre ducks her head, and slips out of the flat nylon collar. Eager to meet the new dog, ignoring Jaylin's call to "come," Fyre bolts. The loose dog snarls and bite's Fyre's neck. Fyre yelps, spins, and tries to run away. The dog bites her hip. Jaylin runs to the dogs. At her approach, the other dog runs away.

In the same way you can't drink water with a fork, you cannot keep a puppy safe or successfully teach her if your training equipment and grooming tools are not correct. Size, material, and function all have a role to play in finding the most effective and appropriate collar, leash, comb, brush, scissors, nail clipper, or nail grinder for your puppy. With the right equipment, if your puppy sees another dog, she cannot slip out of her collar and run away to meet him.

1. Collars

Buckle collars can be flat, rolled, nylon, cloth, or leather. Decorated with stars, embroidered ribbon, stitched with a dog's name, or completely plain, collars serve an important purpose. Buckle collars are the perfect place to hang a dog's license and ID tag. My dogs' ID tags list our telephone number, town, and state. In addition, the ID tag states REWARD. A reward gives people an added incentive to return lost dogs.

My dogs always wear a buckle collar. However, collars twist in carpeting, get caught in another dog's mouth, and catch on bushes and gates. Fit the collar so there is enough space between the collar and the puppy's neck so a puppy's head can slip out easily. This will prevent the puppy from getting trapped in his collar. Buy a collar that you can make bigger than the puppy's current neck size. As puppies grow, their neck size increases. When the current collar no longer has extra room, buy another collar.

Loosely fitted buckle collars are not appropriate for schooling, working, or walking dogs. A puppy's head easily slips out of a loose buckle collar. However, even if I tighten a buckle collar, it does not offer enough physical control or the ability to send a sensitive signal to a puppy. Instead, I use a Pack Leader harness. The triple action of a Pack Leader's body band, chest piece, and neck loop enables me to guide, restrain, protect,

Molly models a Pack Leader harness.

and direct a dog's attention and body. It supports the puppy's body and avoids throwing him off balance. The three-way action prevents the puppy's neck from snapping and does not restrict her leg or shoulder movement. Because it fastens on top of a puppy's withers, the puppy cannot get tangled in a leash if she spins or twists. Also, the puppy cannot reach the leash to bite or chew it. With a simple "tug-and-release" signal, puppies pull less. The signal travels through the neck loop and the chest piece stops the dog's pulling. The puppy's balance shifts to her center under the body band and returns her attention to me. My puppy wears a Pack Leader harness in addition to her buckle collar whenever we walk in the park, work in our backyard, visit a store, or leave our property. It keeps her safe and secure. At home the puppy wears a loose buckle collar that easily slips off her neck if it catches on anything.

I do not recommend "choke" or slip collars with puppies. The puppy's tender neck, throat, and bones can suffer damage or serious injuries. Left unsupervised, puppies who always wear choke collars can get trapped in its grip if the choke collar tightens and twists. In extreme cases, unsupervised puppies hang or twist and die.

2. Leashes

Whether you use a six-foot leash, four-foot leash, long line, or waist leash, the leash needs to fit the size of your puppy. A ¼" nylon leash works perfectly with a Chihuahua, but it is not the right size for a Newfoundland. Always check the size of the leash's hardware. Small puppies do not like large metal snaps clunking under their neck or hitting them in the side of the head or knees. Big strong puppies can break weak plastic fasteners.

A long line gives you control when you start to work distance with a puppy. When I proof a puppy's "come" in an unfenced area, I tie a lightweight, fifteen-foot-long, ¼"-wide climbing rope to her Pack Leader harness. The climbing rope gives me extra strength, which string or nylon cord cannot provide. Jeff stands with the puppy. I call "come." As the puppy runs toward me, the lightweight rope trails behind her. However, if

A ½-inch-wide leash fits a small puppy perfectly.

the puppy decides not to "come," Jeff can easily reach out and grab the rope to prevent her from leaving the area.

A waist leash wraps around your waist. Securely fastened, it allows you to keep the puppy close to you and under observation. However, your hands are free to make dinner, answer the phone, or take out the garbage.

Leashes can be leather, nylon, cotton, or chain. Avoid chain leashes. They are heavy and can injure your hands or hurt your puppy. If you buy a nylon leash, check the edges of it. Rough nylon edges burn if the leash slides too quickly through your hands.

3. Grooming Aids

Grooming gives you the opportunity to check out the puppy's skin, coat, paws, mouth, ears, and eyes. Depending on the breed, brush your puppy at least once a week. Trim the puppy's nails once a week. Overgrown nails spread a dog's pads and prevent smooth contact with the ground. Extra-long nails get hooked in carpet and catch, which could break a nail or injure a toe. Some breeds, such as poodles, bichons frises, and Scottish terriers require professional trimming in addition to your weekly grooming sessions.

Hair coats of different lengths demand different tools. Grooming the flowing coats of my golden retrievers requires three different scissors, two brushes, one comb, and an air dryer. It takes me two hours to bathe, clip, and groom a golden. Grooming the short coat of my Doberman pinscher requires one body clipper, a soft body brush, and a rubber mitt. I bathe and groom Zoe Samantha in a half hour. The type of comb, brush, scissors, clippers, or nail grinder you need depends on the dog. Talk to your breeder, dog groomer, or veterinarian to find the right ones for your puppy. Ask them to teach you the correct way to use your new tools.

Puppies get dirty. They roll in the mud, get blue paws from chewing your son's magic marker, and dried bits of kibble stick to long ears or beards that drag in food dishes. If your puppy swims in a chlorine-filtered swimming pool, bathe the puppy after every swim to prevent dry, itchy, or irritated skin. Before you bathe a puppy, brush him to remove dirt and untangle mats. Brush gently. Puppies do not enjoy rough handling that pulls their skin and tears at their hair coat.

A bath can be as simple as shampoo, hose off, and towel-dry while the puppy stands on the back patio. It can be as elaborate as buying a grooming tub, dog table, and air dryer. Most baths fall somewhere in the middle. If you bathe your puppy in a sink or bathtub, use a rubber mat to provide solid footing and to prevent your puppy from slipping. Then, fill the tub or sink with warm water. The water should reach just under the puppy's belly when you place him in the tub or sink. Ask someone to help you the first few times you bathe a puppy.

Dog shampoos have a different pH balance than human shampoos. Buy a shampoo designed for dogs that does not contain harsh chemicals that dry out a puppy's skin and coat.

Bathing a puppy in a grooming tub.

First, shampoo a dog's back, legs, and tail. Then, start with his back and rinse off the shampoo. Next, rinse the legs, paws, and tail. Do not forget to rinse off the underside of the puppy's paws! If the puppy has a dense hair coat, check that the shampoo and water reaches the skin. After shampooing, rinse it out. One rinse is not enough; even if you think the shampoo is gone, rinse again. Second, shampoo the puppy's head and neck. Before rinsing off his head, cover his eyes with your hand to prevent any soap from entering them. If you do not have an attachable spray nozzle, fill a small pitcher with water. Be careful. Do not allow any suds to enter the puppy's eyes or ears.

To prevent a long-eared dog from getting suds or water in his ears when you wash the ear, close off the ear canal by covering it with your hand. Some people like to place a cotton ball inside the ear canal. If you use a cotton ball, it must be the right size. Do not force or shove it deep into the ear canal. Dogs with erect ears such as Doberman pinschers and schnauzers require a soft cloth or cotton gauze to clean their ears. Find an ear cleaner designed for dogs and use it. Do not probe with cotton swabs inside the dog's ears. If a puppy has excess wax, take your puppy to a dog groomer or veterinarian. Never squirt water into a puppy's ear canals.

Dry your puppy with towels. Then, air-dry, or use an air dryer purchased from a dog supply store to dry the puppy's coat. Do not use your hair dryer. The warm and hot settings are too intense for a dog's coat. Keep the puppy inside until his coat is dry. Wet puppies turned out in cold weather can become chilled. Freshly bathed puppies turned out in warm weather often roll in the grass or dirt.

You're in charge. Training equipment, grooming tools, and bath time help you care for and protect your puppy. Find tools that work for you. Use them. They will keep your puppy safe, happy, and healthy.

Chapter 13

Emeregencies

Plant yourself firmly in the Tao and
you won't ever be uprooted.
Embrace Tao firmly and you won't ever
be separated from it.
Your children will thrive,
and your children's children.[13]

A common refrain runs through this chapter. *See your veterinarian or visit the emergency animal clinic. Call your local or national poison control hotline number.* The time to prepare for an emergency is before it happens. Place your veterinarian's twenty-four-hour emergency animal clinic and local or national poison control (1–888–426–4435) telephone numbers next to the telephone, in your palm pilot, or at any other convenient, easily accessible location. The following information helps you prepare, assess, respond, and support a puppy during an emergency until you can take the puppy to receive medical attention. It is not a substitute for veterinary diagnosis and care.

Emergencies call for immediate action. If a puppy has broken bones, labored breathing, a distended or swollen stomach, burns, seizures, or bleeds from his nose or mouth, bring the puppy to a veterinarian immediately. Six emergencies require immediate veterinary attention: serious trauma, severe pain, shock, difficulty breathing, extensive bleeding, and collapse.

Serious trauma occurs when a puppy is burned, shot, hit by a car, or kicked by a horse. If a dog jumps from a car window, leaps out of a truck bed, or falls from a second-floor deck, pain radiates through his body. Broken bones, gaping wounds, severed or torn arteries, internal injuries, poisoning, and seizures shut down the flow of blood and oxygen to vital organs. Dogs go into "shock." They fall down, weaken, fade, and may lose consciousness. Emergencies demand immediate medical attention.

An injured puppy requires that you stay calm, use a quiet, relaxed voice, and avoid large or wild gestures in order to successfully evaluate the puppy's condition. If a puppy is seriously hurt and in pain, be careful; scared, wounded, pain-filled dogs may bite you. If you cannot work with the puppy safely, call for help. Contact animal care and control, the shelter, or a mobile veterinarian. If the puppy allows you to assess her injuries, the next step is to safely transport her to the veterinarian or emergency clinic. Hold the puppy in your arms or use a box, crate, towel, blanket, or sheet to support her. If you carry the puppy in your arms, place the injured side next to your body. Support her front and rear end with your arms and hands. If a puppy has broken bones, slide a board, heavy piece of cardboard, blanket, or shirt under the dog. Have another person hold the puppy on the board as you move it. If no one can assist you, tape the puppy on the board so she cannot roll off. If you do not have any tape, tear a sheet to make cloth strips. Use common sense. Do not lift a puppy's hind end if you think her back is broken. Call your veterinarian with questions *before* you move the puppy. He may tell you to splint a leg before you transport the dog.

An emergency situation requires you to calmly evaluate the severity of an injury or illness. A one-minute evaluation enables you to check for injuries, decide if the puppy is dehydrated, and observe signs such as bleeding and vomiting.

First, run your eyes over the puppy and her environment.

Look for bleeding, broken bones, vomit, urine, or feces. Check near the puppy for an empty antifreeze container, half-eaten plant, ant bait, rat trap, or anything suspicious-looking or out of the ordinary. Say the puppy's name softly: "Kaylee." Does the puppy respond to her name? She might open her eyes, flick her ears in your direction, or walk to you. If the puppy does not react in any way, say her name again, a little louder. Whistle. Clap your hands. A lack of response on the puppy's part may indicate the puppy is unconscious or in shock.

Second, observe the puppy's breathing.

Watch if the puppy's chest rises and falls. If the chest expands and contracts, the puppy is breathing. If you cannot see the chest move, hold a single tissue in front of the puppy's nostrils. If the tissue moves slightly back and forth, the puppy is breathing. If you do not have a tissue, hold a mirror up to the puppy's nostrils. Breath fogs a mirror. Listen to the puppy's breathing. Breathing that sounds harsh, rapid, jagged, loud, or gasping—or, a total *lack* of breath—calls for emergency action. If the puppy stops breathing, and you know CPR, start it immediately.

Third, evaluate the quality of the heartbeat.

A normal puppy heart rate ranges from 120 to 160 beats per minute until puppies are approximately one year old. To find the pulse, gently lay the puppy down on his side. Gently lift the upper hind leg from the lower hind leg. Do not spread the legs apart if the puppy's back or hind end is injured. High inside the back leg, where the leg meets the body, a valley runs between the two areas. *Lightly* place two fingers in the middle of this valley that runs from front to back. Feel for a pulse to beat against your fingertips. Press gently. If you press too hard, you will not feel a pulse.

If you cannot feel for a pulse on the inner thigh of the puppy's hind leg, look for a pulse by the chest. Lay the puppy down on his right side. Take the puppy's left front elbow in your hand and bend it until it touches the chest. Place your hand under the elbow and next to the chest. Feel for the puppy's heartbeat. To determine the puppy's heart rate, count the puppy's pulse for fifteen seconds and multiply by four seconds.

Conditions Requiring Immediate Veterinary Attention

Bleeding

Bleeding occurs internally or externally. Blood flowing from wounds, bites, or accidents can be seen easily as it spurts out of arteries or streams from lacerations. Continued or severe bleeding requires immediate veterinary attention. Bleeding can also take place internally and accumulate under the skin or inside a dog's body. Even though you do not see blood, a puppy can hemorrhage internally from a fall, injury, fracture, or crushed bones and organs. If you suspect internal bleeding, see your veterinarian immediately.

If you see large and easily removable objects, such as glass or metal pieces, remove them carefully. Do not search for embedded objects in a wound. Then, place a clean pad or towel over the area. Apply direct finger or hand pressure over the area to stop bleeding. If you do not suspect any fractured bones, raise an injured leg so less blood will flow out of the wound. If the wound is small, squeeze it together with your hand as you apply pressure. If the cut is wide and gapes open, it may require wrapping. If a pad or bandage placed on the wound gets soaked with blood, do not remove it. Place another pad on top of it. Never use a tourniquet to stop bleeding.

Severe bleeding involves the rapid loss of blood that occurs from a severed or torn artery. If the blood flows in spurts and does not stop, apply additional pressure with your other hand to the area above the wound that lies between the wound and the heart. If the bleeding flows continuously and does not stop, apply additional pressure with your other hand below the wound. Bleeding that does not quit when you apply direct pressure demands immediate veterinary attention.

Burns

Burns can be caused by chemicals, hot liquids, steam, fire, and electricity. Burns can be superficial or deep. They can cover a small or large area. The skin might be tender, red, swollen, or charred. Run cold water over a burn. Do not soak your puppy in water if the burn covers more than one part of the body. If the area is large or spreads over different body parts, cover the area with a light cold towel or cloth. If you have access to sterile pads, use them. Put ice in a sealed plastic baggie with two table-spoons of salt. The salt lowers the melting point of the ice, allowing the ice to stay colder for a longer amount of time. During the trip to the veteri-narian, place a cloth over the burn and put the ice bag on top of the cloth. Do not let the ice come into direct contact with the burned tissue. Have someone hold it in place. Do not spread ointments, butter, petroleum jelly, or lotion on any burn. Avoid breathing on the burn. See the veterinarian immediately.

Broken Bones

Broken bones can be obvious or subtle. Broken bones stick out through the skin with a compound fracture. In a simple fracture, the bone remains hidden under the skin. If you think a puppy might have a broken bone, do not allow the dog to move. If a puppy's leg juts out at an odd angle or a puppy cannot move or put weight on his leg, call a veterinarian. Describe the puppy's condition and ask how to move the puppy, and whether to wrap or splint the bones.

Drowning

Drowning causes airways to collapse. If a puppy's gums are blue or gray, the blood is not carrying enough oxygen to the tissues. If you know CPR, do it. If a puppy is unconscious, place one hand on each back leg. Raise the puppy's hind end over his head. Another person can cup a hand and gently hit the puppy's chest to expel water. If the puppy regains con-sciousness, bring him to a veterinarian. Fluid can build up in the lungs and cause pneumonia, which can be fatal.

Prevent drowning accidents by placing wire mesh over the fencing that surrounds the swimming pool. The tighter mesh will keep small pup-pies from sneaking through the space between the bars. Lock gates. Teach a puppy how to safely exit from a swimming pool. After a puppy eats, wait one hour before swimming. Limit the number of dives for a ball. Never leave a small puppy alone in a kiddy pool or bathtub. At the lake or ocean, prevent muscle cramps and fatigue by not swimming puppies long distances. Be aware of fast-breaking waves that grab dogs and tow them under the surf. If you take a puppy with you in a boat, have him wear a life preserver designed for dogs. In the winter, never permit a puppy to walk on thin ice that covers lakes or ponds.

Electric Shock

Electric current courses through a puppy's body. Electric shock can damage tissue, stop breathing or heartbeat, and cause unconsciousness. If your puppy has been shocked, turn off the current at the power box. If you cannot stop the current, remove the puppy. Use a nonconductive material such as a wooden broom handle or chair to separate the puppy from the electricity. See your veterinarian.

To prevent a puppy from chewing on electrical cords, remove them. If you cannot take away a cord, coat it with something unpleasant, such as Bitter Apple. Tie up a cord and place it out of reach. Unplug a cord when you are not using it. If you cannot unplug the cord, place it inside a plastic sleeve or tape it on the floor and cover it with a rug. Give your puppy toys, balls, and bones to keep his attention focused on appropriate items to chew.

Frostbite

When puppies freeze their paw pads, ears, or tail, frostbite happens. Frostbite appears as cold, dry, and white areas. Bring the dog inside. Apply warm water compresses (101 to 103 degrees) on the area. Do not use direct heat or rub the area. If the puppy must remain outside, hold him next to your body and cover him with a blanket. Or, place him inside your jacket next to your body. Make a shelter. The puppy needs protection from the wind and cold. Visit the veterinarian as soon as possible.

Heatstroke

Prolonged exposure to heat or hot weather causes heatstroke. The body temperature rises to 104 degrees or higher. Gums are red. The pulse is strong and rapid. There may be vomiting, diarrhea, or total collapse. Bring the puppy into the house or move her into the shade. Spray cool water on her. Drape lightweight, cold, wet towels over the puppy. Turn on a fan so that it blows cool air across the puppy's body. After the puppy's temperature decreases to 104 degrees, take her to the veterinarian. Heatstroke lingers. Even if you lower a puppy's temperature to normal, other conditions such as kidney failure can still develop. A puppy who suffers from heatstroke requires professional medical attention.

Be sensible. If a puppy must be outside during a hot summer day, provide plenty of shade and water. Keep exercise to a minimum. Do not take a puppy for a long run in hot weather. Never leave a puppy in a parked car.

Hypothermia

Leaving a puppy locked outside in the pouring rain without adequate shelter, allowing him to swim in spring-fed or glacier lakes, cross chilly, deep, wide creeks, or romp in snowdrifts for long periods of time, can cause hypothermia. A puppy's body temperature drops after prolonged exposure to cold. A weak pulse, shivering, and decreased heart rate indicates hypothermia. Puppies stumble. Activity decreases, drowsiness develops, and the potential for collapse increases. Bring the dog inside. Check for frostbite. Then, hold the puppy next to your body, or cover the puppy with warm towels. Do not use direct heat or rub an area. Bring the puppy to your veterinarian.

Poisoning

Poisoning occurs when puppies eat and swallow something harmful to their system, such as toilet bowl cleaner, weed killer, or insect sprays. If you suspect your puppy has swallowed something toxic, read the label, call your veterinarian, or contact the national poison control center (1–888–426–4435). If you do not know what the puppy ate and the puppy has vomited, bring the vomit with you in a sealed plastic bag to the veterinarian. Do not induce vomiting unless your veterinarian tells you it's necessary.

Poisoning is not limited to what puppies eat. Snake, scorpion, and spider bites, and bee, wasp, and jellyfish stings also introduce harmful toxins to a puppy's body. If you think the puppy has been stung or bitten by a snake, restrict your puppy's movement. Do not try to suck out venom with your mouth or place ice on the bite. Never use a tourniquet. Carry the puppy to the car and drive straight to a veterinarian.

Shock

When vital organs do not receive the flow of blood and oxygen they need, shock results. A weak, rapid pulse; gray gums; unfocused eyes; and shallow breathing are signs of shock. Puppies collapse from severe trauma, bleeding, and allergic reactions. If a puppy goes into shock, first stop any bleeding and close any wounds. Then, wrap the puppy in a blanket or towel. If you know CPR and your puppy needs it, do it. Transport the puppy to your veterinarian. You should expect shock and be ready to provide treatment for it when any serious injury occurs. Treatment for shock is more successful if initiated before symptoms appear.

IMPORTANT SKILLS, KNOWLEDGE, AND SUPPLIES

How to Use a Rectal Thermometer

A normal temperature ranges from 100 degrees to 102.5 degrees. Contact and visit a veterinarian if a temperature is below 100 degrees or over 104 degrees. Thermometers can be digital or mercury. Mercury thermometers must be coated with petroleum jelly or a water-based lubricant before insertion.

Step 1. Stand the puppy or ask the puppy to lie down.

With a mercury thermometer, hold the plain glass end in your hand. Snap your wrist twice to shake down the mercury column below 95 degrees.

Step 2. Place petroleum jelly or a water-based lubricant on the end with the mercury.

Step 3. Insert the thermometer into the puppy's rectum until it reaches the start of the mercury. Do not hold the end of the thermometer in place with your hands; that will affect the temperature.

Step 4. Wait three minutes.

Step 5. Gently pull out the thermometer and read the number where the mercury stops. The number is the puppy's temperature.

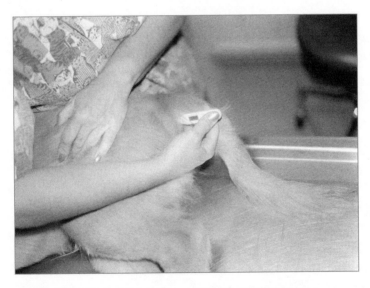

A veterinary technician takes a puppy's temperature.

How to Use a Digital Thermometer

Step 1. Insert the thermometer until it just passes the tip.

Step 2. The thermometer beeps when it determines the puppy's temperature.

Step 3. Pull it out and read the number. The displayed number is the puppy's temperature.

How to Take a Pinch Test

A pinch test determines if a puppy is dehydrated. Take a fold of skin between your thumb and middle finger on the side of the chest or at the top of the neck. Pinch your fingers together. Within one to two seconds, the skin should lay flat. If the skin takes longer than two seconds, or stays pinched, the puppy may be dehydrated.

A pinch test is not effective with skinny or overweight puppies. Instead, you must use their gums as an indicator. Lift up the puppy's lip and feel the gums. Dry, sticky gums often indicate that a puppy is dehydrated. Do not take any chances with dehydration. See the veterinarian.

Typical Color of Gums and Lips

Normal gums are pink. Lift up a puppy's lip. If the gums are pale pink, blue, gray, bright red, brown, or white, call the veterinarian. If a puppy normally has black gums and lips, observe the color of the lower eyelid's membrane. Use your index finger to lightly pull the skin away from the lower eyelid. Look inside at the membrane to see its color. Pink indicates that circulation is normal. If you see another color, contact your veterinarian.

Canine First-aid Kit

Every home should include three puppy first-aid kits. Keep one kit in the kitchen, store another kit in the car, and carry one kit with you when you hike, sail, or swim. Remember, find places to store the first-aid kits where puppies and children cannot reach them. Inside the kit place scissors, tweezers, needle-nose pliers, two-inch roll of gauze, sterile pads, vet wrap, canine rectal thermometer, water-based lubricant, Benadryl, eye wash, hypoallergenic adhesive tape, nylon leash, compact thermal blanket, latex gloves, towel, and small flashlight or penlight. In the kit include the telephone numbers of your veterinarian, the twenty-four-hour animal emergency clinic, the national poison hotline number, along with a list of any medications your puppy currently takes.

Bert and Marshall, sixty-two-year-old twin brothers, live on a small ranch next to a twenty-thousand-acre desert preserve. Emily, a seven-month-old Rhodesian ridgeback, is the newest member of their family. Emily races Bert out to the corrals when he feeds the cattle. She eats horse-hoof clippings when Marshall trims their feet. Emily explores the sandy wash that runs through their property. At night she lies on the back porch watching for squirrels and rabbits to chase.

In the desert after a summer rain, toads the size of baseballs come out of their hiding places. They sit under porch lights and backyard spotlights waiting for insects, attracted by the light, to bask in the artificial "sun." Dinner under the stars. Every night, the yard light beckons; the toads know it, and wait for dinner to appear.

At 9:00 P.M. on Saturday night, Bert walks outside to fetch Emily. He sees Emily walking head down, with wobbly legs, foam cascading from her mouth. He aims his flashlight at her face. Two toad legs dangle from her lips. Calling for Marshall, he runs to Emily, pries open her mouth, and removes a fat, limp toad body.

"Marshall, get the hose. Turn on the water. Emily's grabbed a poisonous toad."

Short, quick steps bring the hose to Bert. Marshall aims a steady stream of water across the inside of Emily's mouth to avoid flushing the toxins down her throat. Three minutes later Emily's drooling stops. Then, she shakes her head and moves slowly back into the house.

Bert's knowledge saved Emily's life. He knew the signs of poisoning, knew how to clear toad poison from a dog's mouth, and he reacted calmly. Bert stayed centered in tao and maintained his composure. His mind focused clearly. Bert acted with confidence because he knew how to deal with a toad's toxic body before it permanently damaged Emily.

The more you know, the more help you can give in an emergency. Study and practice before an emergency strikes. Attend a dog first-aid class. Learn CPR. Ask your veterinarian to show you how to take a pulse and read a thermometer. Keep a first-aid kit on hand. Quick, calm emergency care prevents a situation from getting worse. Your care, comfort, and support can save a puppy's life.

Part 3 | The Way of Learning

Chapter 14
The Space Inside the Pitcher Makes It Valuable

A friend of mine loves to sit at a potter's wheel and turn moist, brown lumps of clay into plates, cups, bowls, vases, pitchers, and the occasional water fountain. I am fascinated when, under her expert hands, a lump of clay turns into a pitcher. Her fingers support the clay, while her thumbs dig deep and curve out the sides. Then, with a gentle pull, she draws up the clay. The wheel stops. Her index finger and middle finger press together to form the lip. A delicate touch, and a spout appears. She fastens a handle to the pitcher's side. It's finished. After drying, firing, and glazing, the pitcher is ready for use. The empty space inside a pitcher is essential for its purpose.

A puppy's mind is like the space inside a pitcher. Her inner thoughts—mental attitude, emotional outlook, and knowledge—affect how she acts. As the puppy acquires new information, facts, and skills, her behavior changes.

Working with the canine brain is the key to raising a good dog. Every time a puppy barks, runs away, chews, digs, sits, heels, cowers, jumps, or bites, you see the result of what she thinks. Dogs think, decide, and act.

Puppies make decisions all the time. There is a direct link between what a dog thinks and how she behaves. When you call "come," a puppy chooses whether or not she will return to you. As leader of the pack, you work with a puppy's inner nature, teach new skills, develop a puppy's thinking ability, and reward correct decisions.

Learning is a journey filled with cognitive challenges. Acquiring skills and knowledge requires puppies to engage their brain, not just their body. In our house we do not have a doggy door. Our dogs must signal to us their need to eliminate. Logan rings a bell that hangs on the doorknob. Zoe Samantha licks my hand. Red Sun Rising stands and stares at me. Jet barks softly. Four different ways to communicate, "Please take me outside now." As soon as we see, hear, or feel a signal, we take them outside to do their business under the trees. When the canine brain engages, puppies ring bells, lick hands, stand and stare, or bark to communicate what they need. Three events indicate when a puppy's awareness turns into mastery.

1) A puppy performs an action quickly and easily.

2) A puppy remembers what he has learned.

3) A puppy performs a requested behavior at any time or place.

Behavior that requires a puppy to modify his natural instincts requires his canine brain to engage. A puppy that lives in a home without a doggy door must learn how to indicate that he needs a bathroom break. As a puppy, Logan's inner nature dictates that a full bladder means *urinate now*. My task is to teach Logan new ideas and behaviors: wait to eliminate, signal me, and urinate and defecate outside.

The first stage requires that Logan learn elimination occurs outside—not inside—the house. Every time Logan urinates or defecates in the backyard, he earns a reward. As Logan urinates, I repeat softly, "Go tinkle. Go tinkle. Good boy." When Logan finishes, I give him a food reward. When Logan defecates, I repeat softly, "Go poop. Go poop. Good boy." When Logan finishes, I give him a food reward.

During the second stage, Logan discovers that ringing a bell results in me opening the door to the backyard. I attach a 5-inch red, jingle bell to the doorknob. The length of the string permits the bell to rest at the same height as Logan's nose.

Puppies usually need to go out as soon as they wake up, after they play, and after they eat. It's easy to stand by the door at those times and say, "Logan outside? Do you need to go tinkle?" The first day I ring the bell before I say, "Outside? Logan, go tinkle." The second day I hold the string so the bell hangs approximately two inches away from the door. Logan's nose brushes and rings the bell as he walks past it. The third day I place a small dot of peanut butter on the bell. I stand next to the door and call, "Logan, Logan." When Logan runs up, I say, "Logan, do you want to go outside? Let's go tinkle." I stare at the bell and wiggle it slightly so that the bell moves, but it does not ring. Logan follows my eyes, sees the bell, smells the peanut butter, and touches the bell with his nose. The bell rings. One quick tongue lick and the peanut butter disappears. I quickly snap the leash to Logan's collar, open the door, and we walk outside.

I say "Go tinkle" and Logan walks under the tree and squats. *Success.* Logan earns a reward. After a few more bells with peanut butter, Logan eagerly rings the bell. He quickly and easily learns to associate a physical feeling—the need to eliminate—with a new behavior: ringing a bell.

Logan demonstrates his new skill when we stay at a motel. I tie a bell to the doorknob. Logan rings the bell. I take him outside. Traveling with Logan is effortless.

Awareness turns into mastery when puppies make the connection be-tween what they know and how they act, remember what they learn, and change their behavior accordingly. Logan demonstrates his mastery when he rings the bell in a new location, without any prompting from me, to sig-nal his desire to go outside to eliminate.

Knowing what is enough is freedom.
Knowing when to stop is safety.
Practice these and you'll endure.[14]

Working with a puppy's mind is a delicate art. Allow your intuition to guide you; then, you will know when to push and ask the puppy to "down-stay" for twenty more seconds, or when to pause and take a play break.

Ron takes a play break with Gidget.

Watch the puppy's behavior. During a five-minute schooling session, a five-month-old Shiba Inu that stops working with you and starts chasing squirrels demonstrates that when a brain gets tired, the body takes a break. That's normal behavior. Think about it. When you work or learn something new, your mind also wears out.

Six practices will help you make the most out of each schooling session:

1. Work in a quiet area. Keep distractions to a minimum.

2. Plan schooling sessions before mealtime.

3. Train in short sessions.

4. Use rewards.

5. Focus on one idea or behavior at a time.

6. Pause, take breaks, rest, relax, and play during schooling sessions.

1. Work in a quiet area. Keep distractions to a minimum.

Find a quiet work space for you and the puppy. Close the door to the family room and create a private schooling area. School the puppy outside in the backyard. Or, practice inside the house, garage, or basement. Turn off the radio and television. If your children want to participate, ask them to sit quietly and watch. After the puppy understands how to sit, down, come, and walk quietly on a leash, they can help you work with the puppy.

Gradually increase the type and intensity of distractions. School the puppy in front of visitors. Work the puppy while the children play. Visit a park or store and ask the puppy to focus on you. A puppy's attention span depends on the situation. It is much harder for a puppy to pay attention to you when children practice soccer in the backyard. In the beginning, teach in a quiet space.

2. Plan schooling sessions before mealtime.

I am convinced that puppies are born with invisible tiny watches on their front paws. Puppies know when it is time for breakfast, lunch, dinner, and late evening meals. Puppies love to eat, and they must eat to support their growing bodies. A perfect time to school puppies is before mealtime. Puppies are hungry. Use this natural drive to your advantage. Behavior-contingent food rewards speed a puppy's desire to "sit," "stay," or have his nails clipped.

3. Train in short sessions.

Puppies have short attention spans. Try ten-second, thirty-second, one-minute, and five-minute schooling sessions. Fit schooling sessions into your routine. Practice "down" and "sit" while you brush your teeth. Practice "down-stay" while you load the dishwasher. Ask a puppy to "sit" before you feed breakfast, "down" before lunch, or "shake" before dinner. Let the puppy's learning and your teaching seamlessly flow into each other.

4. Use rewards.

We reward puppies by our actions. We pet them; throw balls; play with toys; convey feelings of pride, love, happiness, or excitement; and give them food (cheese, hot dogs, or soft liver snacks). We indicate our approval of a puppy's behavior with words: "Yes," "good boy," "excellent," "super," "fine," or sounds (whistles, clicks, beeps, clucking mouth noises).

5. Focus on one idea or behavior at a time.

Try this: Sit in a chair and with the point of your right foot, draw a clockwise circle. Easy. Now for the hard part: At the same time you draw a clockwise circle with your foot, take your right hand and draw a counterclockwise circle in the air. Can't do it? Frustrated? Keep trying.

In the same way you cannot draw two circles in opposite directions, training more than one aspect of a behavior at a time confuses and frustrates puppies. For example, when you teach "stay," focus on increasing your physical distance from the puppy, *or*, increasing the amount of time you expect the puppy to "stay." However, do not increase your distance and also increase the amount of time you expect the puppy to "stay" during the same practice session.

6. Pause, take breaks, rest, relax, and play during schooling sessions.

There is a time to act and a time to wait. Puppies experience information overload just like you do. Puppy brains and bodies use pauses, breaks, rests, and playtime to refresh, reenergize, integrate, and override automatic reactions. A time-out gives puppies time to merge what they have learned into what they *know*.

Puppies are smart, creative, and inventive because they use their minds. Your challenge is to stimulate a canine brain to think, process information, and learn. Then, your puppy will not chase the cat or eat the roast beef that sits on the counter, because his mind says "no."

Chapter 15
Silent Training

The best leader is one whose existence
is barely known.
Next best is one who is loved and praised.
Next is one who is feared.
Worst of all is a leader who is despised.
If you fail to trust people,
they won't turn out to be trustworthy.
Therefore, guide others by quietly relying on Tao.
Then, when the work is done, the people can say,
'We did this ourselves.'[15]

Ellen fell in love at a pet store. On her way to buy a new bedspread at
Macy's, she passed by Pets R Us. Three slick-coated brindle and fawn
puppies were running and leaping in a doggy play area behind a large
glass wall. Ellen walked into the store, leaned over the playpen, and the
brindle puppy ran to her outstretched hand. She scooped him up, held
him next to her chest, and he licked her face. There was no doubt in her
mind. "Harley" was coming home with her today.

Two weeks later, Ellen cannot imagine her life without Harley. He
sleeps with her. They watch television together. He wears a cute little biker
outfit that Ellen bought him. Before Harley, Ellen's life was dull and boring. Now Ellen plays with Harley, walks with Harley, and snuggles with
Harley on the couch.

Harley makes Ellen happy—wildly, deliriously happy. Harley runs to
greet Ellen when she comes in with the Sunday newspaper or after taking

out the garbage. He lies at her feet while she eats at the kitchen table. He leaps on her lap and gives her "kisses." Ellen found her soul mate when Harley roared into her life.

Ellen loves Harley. However, love without leadership brings chaos. To keep their relationship running smoothly, Ellen must learn how to be leader of their pack.

Leaders who follow tao, go first as guides. They support, shape, establish, maintain, and reinforce. They take a stand without turning it into a confrontation. They understand that if they are pushy, overbearing, or combative, leading becomes unnatural.

Puppies defy, disobey, and ignore your requests in response to unreasonable force, artificial rules, and unrealistic expectations. It is the difference between discipline and boundaries. Discipline insists; boundaries exist.

> When cleverness and intellect abound,
> people don't do well.
> A leader who governs with cleverness
> cheats his people.
> A leader who governs with simplicity
> is a blessing to his people.
> These are two alternatives.
> Understanding them is subtle insight.
> The use of subtle insight brings
> all things back into the oneness.[16]

Leaders understand that how they act affects what happens next. Aware of pack behavior, drives, and instincts, they do not interfere with the natural order. Instead, they work with a puppy's inner nature and show puppies new ways to fetch, walk, and jump. In the process, a leader's position is established and her authority is accepted. When puppies are allowed to express their inner nature, they learn faster, respond quicker, develop self-control, and mature into good dogs. You get what you want: a good dog. And they get what they want: to be a dog.

Silent training works with the natural order of events and bridges the gap between dogs and people. It is the gentle art of pack leadership, where actions speak louder than words. To establish yourself as "leader of the pack," become silent. Then you will not fight against a puppy's instincts and drives, but work with them. Committed to the pack, you know what to do. Part of the pack, your way is accepted.

Ellen does not know enough about canine behavior to give Harley the love and leadership he requires. Raising a puppy without learning about canine nature is like placing a ladder on ice. Although the ladder rests against the shed, the ladder can slide or fall if the ice cracks, shifts, or melts while being used. In the same way, you cannot design successful lessons or make smart decisions if your feet are not firmly planted on the ground. The best footing for understanding dogs is to learn about the way of the pack. Then, you can use your increased knowledge about pack behavior, drives, and body language to communicate with your puppy in a way that he naturally understands.

A pack is a social group that bonds together for survival and safety. Pack members need and support each other. Specific rituals and daily routines establish a social hierarchy where higher rank carries more privileges. Every day and throughout the day, pack members check and re-check pack order. The dynamics of the pack demand it.

The study of wolves, dogs' closest relatives, helps us understand pack behavior. In the pack, the alpha female, or "first female," breeds and determines the role of other females in the pack. The alpha dog, or "first dog," guards territory, deals with rivals, repels strangers, forages for food, eats first, and maintains order between pack members. Alpha dogs control lower-ranking dogs by using specific body language, gaits, and facial expressions. The alpha dog stands erect with a high head and tail carriage.

He may turn his head to the side, exposing his throat, when other pack members meet him. He walks confidently. Frequently, the entire pack gathers around the alpha dog at his return.

The alpha dog dominates and controls the pack without lethal confrontations. The survival of the pack depends on his ability to command without resorting to force. Only healthy, uninjured wolves can help him track, stalk, and kill game.

Wolves communicate their dominance or subservience through specific body language. Pack members want to be part of the group, so they tolerate, submit, and cooperate. Ritualized behaviors maintain the pack's stability. Lower-ranking wolves display submissive behaviors to prevent aggressive acts. They crouch, crawl, or cower; a lower head and body shows deference. Averted eyes, tucked or low tail, and licking their lips indicate a lower status. Lower-ranking members defer to each other and to the pack leader. Conflicts are settled through displays of deference from lower-ranking members. Loyal to the leader, they follow his lead, repelling lone wolves or tracking game.

The way of the pack requires wolves to cooperate with each other. Respect and recognition of the alpha, ritualized greeting ceremonies, and appropriate body language and gestures maintain the social hierarchy. Three basic drives motivate wolves in their survival dance: pack, prey, and defense. Self preservation depends on their ability to hunt, mate, and defend against rivals or intruders.

PACK DRIVE

Wolves band together. Pack drive encourages bonds among group members so they can hunt, mate, and repel strangers and intruders. Rituals and routines maintain the social hierarchy. A higher rank carries more privileges. Submissive behaviors show that lower-ranking members acknowledge their place in the pack and accept it. Position, place, body language, facial expression, and gait indicate status in the pack and maintain the wolves' power structure. Pack drive stimulates, motivates, and compels cooperation. It enables the pack to function seamlessly as a team, without effort.

PREY DRIVE

Survival requires eating. Prey drive involves searching, tracking, stalking, chasing, and killing game.

DEFENSE DRIVES

Defense/Fight Drive

Defense/Fight surfaces when wolves protect their territory from other packs or individuals. Wolves also fight to determine alpha position in the pack.

Defense/Flight Drive

Defense/Flight appears when wolves leave rather than face a challenging situation. In extreme cases, they freeze. Unable to move, they cower, turn belly up, cover their belly with their tail, and wet themselves.

Dogs inherit pack behavior, drives, and instincts from their ancient wolf ancestors. They demonstrate many wolfish traits. Given the opportunity, dogs choose to live, eat, and travel together. They willingly spend a significant portion of the day near each other. Although most dogs are not as sensitive or extreme in their reactions as wolves, innate drives impel them to hunt, search for a mate, protect territory, and rebuff rivals. The strength of canine drives determines how willing they are to participate in our human/canine pack.

Pack drive dictates the amount of cooperation dogs offer, and their willingness to accept their position in the pack. In border collies, we call it "biddable." We want "biddable" dogs who will listen to our direction when they herd sheep, perform an agility course, or chase a cat. Will our border collie follow our bidding, fight against it, or remain aloof? Depending on the amount of pack drive in our border collies, the answer changes.

The strength of pack drive is demonstrated by the amount of physical contact with people that canines seek, accept, or reject. Puppies that are high in pack drive follow you around the house and in the yard. They want you to pet them. When you teach them, they try to please you. Puppies high in pack drive want to work with you. They do not wander far away, but stay near you. Can they chase a cat? Sure, but when you call them, they run back to you. They take their direction from their leader, and the leader's attitude affects their ease or comfort in new situations. Puppies high in pack drive stick with you.

Prey drive governs the ability to stalk, hunt, and eat game. Survival requires that dogs eat. In the human/canine pack, puppies no longer have to search for food and kill game. However, stalking, hunting, and killing behaviors still show up in dogs.

We see prey drive in puppies when they pounce, shake, and "kill" their toys. They sniff shoes searching for scents. They track the smell of wild rabbits that run through bushes and into flower gardens. Puppies high in prey drive run after kids on bicycles or chase cars. They bury their bones in the yard or under the sofa cushions. The intensity of prey drive is indicated by the amount of their chasing, barking, jumping, biting, carrying, or shaking and destroying toys.

Rebecca has an Australian shepherd who delightedly brings his trophies home. Inside the house, tormented lizards are forced to play a wild game of "catch and release" until Rebecca secures their safety. Will the Aussie chase a cat? Yes. When Rebecca calls him, it depends on the intensity of the "chase" whether he will return to her.

Dogs defend. Self-preservation depends on their ability to fight, run away, or freeze. The intensity of their defensive drive determines which action they choose. Max, a nineteen-week-old Bouvier des Flandres, hates being picked up, bites at the brush when Esther tries to groom him, and lunges at the veterinary technician when she picks up his paws to trim his nails. Dogs with high fight drive growl when you try to take a toy away from them. They stare at you with hard eyes, and hackles raise high on their shoulders. They lie in front of the main entrance to your house and guard entrances to bedrooms by lying in open doorways. They watch, observe, and guard. They dislike grooming and don't enjoy being touched. Will they chase a cat? You bet. And sometimes the cat dies. When you call them, will they return to you? It depends. If they see you as their leader, they will come.

Kansas is a rescue border collie mix. After Meg and Tom brought her home, she lived under their front deck for three weeks. They enticed her out from under the deck by placing her food dish a little closer to the back door every day. Eventually, she crept inside the house. Now Kansas eats in their kitchen. During the day she hides under their bed. If they watch television, Kansas creeps, belly low, almost touching the carpet, on a curving path to join them. However, if Tom stands suddenly, Kansas runs and hides under the bed.

Canines with high flight drive avoid confrontations by running away. They hide under a bed, in a crate, or run out through a doggy door. Bending over to pick them up, a loud voice, or a stranger can cause them to submissively urinate. When they can't find a way out, they often freeze. They hide. Will they chase a cat? Yes, as long as the cat doesn't turn around, hiss, and scratch them on the nose. Can you call them? Yes; they understand a social hierarchy, know their place in it, and willingly take direction as long as they feel safe.

Silent training enables us to work with a dog's natural behavior, drives, and instincts by recognizing the importance of pack, prey, and defense drives. Silent trainers practice wu wei and work with a dog's inner nature. By following the way of the pack, they follow the natural order and establish themselves as leader. Silent leaders do not fight against canine instincts, but reinforce them. They lead by understanding a subtle canine hierarchy that values specific positions, places, features, or movements that confer status. Leaders who follow the way of the pack influence puppies by their behavior. They do not force, apply pressure, or demand. Instead, they follow tao teachings that explain how to act sparingly from inner stillness.

I remember when Red Sun Rising, my ten-month-old golden retriever, tested the strength of his legs and leapt over the garden wall while we were outside. Red ran down the drive and across the road. I yelled his name and whistled. He stopped and looked. As pack leader, I turned my back on Red, shouted "come," and Red ran to me. He sniffed my hand. I turned my head away. Then I stared into his eyes. Red licked his lips. We ran and played in celebration at his return. When Red ran back to me, I wanted to yell and berate him for leaving the yard, because I was scared. He could have been hit by a car. However, as leader, I remained silent, accepted his offerings of respect, and played with him. As Red licked my hand, I knew this moment defined our future relationship.

Silence is bigger than me, mine, or yours. When we are silent, our definition of pack and family expands. As leader, we travel tao's invisible pathways that link us to our puppy. Four practices demonstrate pack order, underline your importance as a pack leader, and establish you as a silent trainer.

Practice #1. Act like a leader.

Practice #2. Establish a greeting ritual.

Practice #3. Develop a buddy system.

Practice #4. Reinforce behavior.

Practice #1. Act like a leader.

Leaders establish, shape, maintain, and reinforce. Leaders who follow tao practice wu wei, work with the inner nature of puppies, and follow the natural order. They establish themselves as "first" in the social hierarchy. As leader they determine when and how puppies eat; go first through doorways and gates; control access to bedrooms, toys, and their personal space; start and end games; and expect respect. They become leader by acting like "first dog."

1. Eat first.

In a pack, the leader always eats first. You can eat your meal first and then feed the puppy. However, eating first is not always convenient. On the days when your husband comes home late, your daughter has soccer practice, and you have a meeting to attend, you can still demonstrate your rank as leader. It's easy. Set the dog dish on the counter. Next to it, place a small plate for you. Your plate must be next to the puppy's dish on the counter. Place a cookie, cracker, three grapes, or an apple on your plate. While the puppy watches, eat. After you finish eating, feed the puppy.

Remember, in the canine social hierarchy, position and place determine status. Taking an apple out of the refrigerator and casually munching on it as you wander or talk on the telephone is not the same as locating the "kill"—i.e., your plate and the puppy dish—standing next to them, and eating first.

If a puppy wanders away before eating all her food, pick up the bowl after ten minutes pass. Do not leave leftover food for her to snack on during the day. As leader, you determine when the puppy eats. Most puppies eat their meals quickly. Eating fast originates from hungry wolf ancestors who knew the wolf that ate the fastest ate the most food.

2. Go first.

Leaders operate from the front of the pack. Go first when you walk through doorways, through a gate, and up or down the stairs. The alpha must be in front to protect, hunt, or defend.

The easiest way to go first is to restrict or deny access to bedrooms, great rooms, or decks. Close the doors so you walk through first.

In one home I installed a wrought iron gate at the top of the stairs to restrict access to the second floor. Closed doors or baby-gates establish that you control where the puppy goes in your house. Leaders control territory. By limiting access, puppies depend on you. They recognize you as leader because you control where they range.

Forcing puppies to sit and stay while you walk through a door does not prove you are the pack leader. Puppies may execute your signals perfectly, but that does not mean they accept and recognize your leadership. However, if a puppy backs up a few steps and waits while you open the door and walk through, you know they accept your position as "first dog." Puppies who defer to the leader willingly step back without any encouragement or signals from you, so that you can lead the way.

Puppies need to learn that doors and gates control access. To teach your puppy how to defer to you at a door, walk up to a closed door. Stand in front of it. If the puppy backs up naturally behind you, open the door, and walk through while the puppy trails after you.

If a puppy pushes at the door and crowds your feet, wait quietly. Frequently, puppies get bored when nothing exciting happens and leave. When your puppy turns around and starts to walk away, open the door and walk through. The puppy will feel you move and follow after you.

If you start to open a door and the puppy runs in front of you, quickly close the door. You can shut a door rapidly if you crack it open and it does not swing wide. You must move fast. You do not want to hit the puppy's head with the door or squeeze his body between the door and the wall. Instead, you want to teach the puppy that doors restrict access, and as leader, you control the door. Puppies that wait for leaders to go first show respect, deference, and self-control.

Dogs understand the concept of territory. They bark when the meter reader walks in the side yard to read the meter. They defecate or urinate to mark boundaries. After my border collie Pip eliminates, she scratches long furrows in the ground as a visual and scent signal to indicate her territory. Doorways present a perfect opportunity to demonstrate that as leader, you control access. A puppy learns that their freedom to roam, run, and explore depends on you.

Dogs know that position and place indicate status in the pack. Leaders do not move around or over a sleeping dog, but require a puppy to move out of their way. They do not allow puppies to lie in front of a busy hallway, at the main entrance to the house, on landings, or at the top of stairs. Remember, you can use baby-gates, wrought iron gates, or closed doors to control a puppy's freedom. Puppies learn that only leaders freely go anywhere they want.

Dogs understand that the higher the position, the higher the rank. Leaders do not allow puppies on couches, beds, chairs, or ottomans. They realize that puppies belong below, underneath, and on the periphery.

Leaders make a point of sitting where the puppy sits or sleeps—on his bed, in a corner, or next to the sofa. They understand that leaders control territory by associating specific places with their presence, so they sit where their puppy sits, rests, or sleeps. If you avoid sitting, laying, or spending time in a puppy's area, it could cause the puppy to misunderstand his place in your pack.

For example, our Doberman, Zoe Samantha, has a fine, sparse, red, "Dobe" hair coat. Zoe chills easily. To keep her warm during cold winter nights, we wrap her in a peach comforter to create a cozy, warm, sleeping den. After we get up in the morning, we fold the peach comforter into a neat square that sits on the floor in our bedroom. All of our dogs love to sit and sleep on Zoe's comforter. I make a point of sitting on the comforter at least once a week. If another dog is lying on it as I sit down, the dog moves out of my way. As I sit there our dogs come up to sniff and greet me. They lie quietly near me, respecting my space and place as their leader.

Leaders also control territory by their ability to touch a puppy's body anywhere—feet, belly, ears, mouth, tail, and body. They give tummy rubs. They stroke their hands along the top of the puppy's neck, withers, and shoulders—an easy way to indicate their status as "first dog."

3. Start and stop all games.

If a puppy comes up to you with a toy in his mouth, turn and look away. "Not now," your body language says. Thirty seconds later, with a toy of your choosing, ask the puppy to play. As "first dog," after you finish playing, keep the toy. Do not drop the toy on the floor after you finish playing! Instead, put the toy in a closet, drawer, or cupboard, out of puppy range.

If a puppy grabs your shoe or glove and plays keep-away, it's not a game. Turn your back. Walk away. If you chase after the puppy, you lose. By ignoring the puppy and leaving the area, you demonstrate that you determine the games you play. Puppies often steal shoes and other items to get our attention. If we ignore them, the impetus for them to take our things disappear. Instead, pay attention to your puppy and initiate play with her. Then, she will not need to steal a shoe to get your attention.

4. Expect respect.

Expect your puppy to defer to you as leader of the pack. However, a puppy can't treat you as leader if you don't act like one. Your behavior must show the puppy that you are first in all ways. Then the puppy will defer to you. Puppies only resist when they don't respect their leader.

Practice #2. Establish a greeting ritual.

Dale has an older Belgian sheepdog and a seven-month-old rottweiler and golden retriever mix. She brings them over to my house for play sessions with Red, our ten-month-old golden retriever. Dale, Jeff, and I watch them meet, greet, and play. I am fascinated by how they communicate with each other by a bark, bow, or blink of an eye. Dogs use greeting rituals to demonstrate pack order in the same way as their wolf ancestors. Wolves reestablish the social hierarchy after a separation from their leader. Dale's Belgian and rottie-retriever mix and our golden retriever also establish who is leader when they reunite.

There is no doubt when we watch them interact that the Belgian is "first dog." The other dogs approach her. She turns her head and sniffs the ground. She remains aloof with a high head, body, and tail carriage as they lick her muzzle. Satisfied, she moves away. She walks the perimeter of my agility ring while the other two dogs play.

We can also use a greeting ritual to demonstrate our position as pack leader. It's simple. When you return home after work, a trip to the store, a short visit with your neighbors, or any separation where an opaque closed door separates you and the puppy, after you walk into the house, stay silent. Do not talk, touch, or look at the puppy. As pack leader, walk calmly and confidently into the house. Sit down at the kitchen counter or dining room table. In the beginning, do not move around. Sit quietly. Scan a magazine article or talk on the telephone, but keep an eye on the puppy. At first the puppy will do the "doggy dance." She will nuzzle your hand, bring you a toy, or jump on your legs to entice you to pay attention to her. However, act like a leader and ignore her. If she leaps in your lap, gently remove her without talking or looking at her. Place her on the ground.

As soon as the puppy accepts you as leader, her behavior changes. Instead of running, leaping, or nuzzling your hands, she lies down. In order to establish your leadership, wait until she lies down for three consecutive minutes, and then call her name. Say "Frida, come." Feed her a treat after she runs to you. Now play, touch, talk, and snuggle with your puppy.

If the puppy gets up before three minutes pass, wait for her to lie down again. Use your watch; time it. The first few times you practice this greeting ritual, it might take ten or fifteen minutes before the puppy lies down for three minutes. However, if you are consistent, the puppy will learn quickly to lie and wait for the leader's signal.

Any time the puppy and you are separated, and the puppy is not physically confined in a crate or x-pen, reestablish your leadership by using this greeting ritual. If you work at home or it's the weekend, create times when you "leave" by walking into the garage and closing the door, taking out the garbage, or picking up the mail. The more times you repeat the greeting ritual, the easier it is for the puppy to understand that you are leader.

Remember, if a puppy stays in a crate, x-pen, laundry room, or kitchen when you are not home, immediately take her outside so she can eliminate before you practice the greeting ritual. However, do not chat, touch, or fuss over her. Quietly, ask her to "go potty." After she eliminates, return to the house. Walk inside with her. Then, leave. Walk out the front, back, or side door. Close it. Wait approximately thirty seconds. Then, return and practice the greeting ritual.

The greeting ritual accomplishes three important ideas in the dog's mind. First, you are pack leader. Second, it teaches a puppy to "come." Third, the leader controls food. You reward the puppy for returning to you with a food treat.

Practice #3. Develop a buddy system.

In swimming, horseback riding, and hiking, I use a "buddy system." A "buddy" is someone who looks out for your best interests. A buddy knows where you are, what you do, and helps you. A canine "buddy system" allows you to establish leadership, show a puppy that a specific behavior is inappropriate, and give a dog time to pause, think, and make a different choice. It brings out the best in your puppy. The buddy system is based on canine behavior. Mothers grab puppies by the scruff of the neck to carry them. In the canine social hierarchy, a dominant dog rests his head, places his mouth, or lifts a paw over another dog's neck, withers, and shoulder area. We can accomplish a similar act of leadership by bending over and taking a silent *gentle* hold of a puppy's collar.

If your puppy barks at another dog, "buddy up." Quietly hold the puppy's collar when he starts barking. Do not talk, look, or touch him. Refuse to feel angry, upset, or frustrated. Leaders are calm. Stand still. Bend over, hold the puppy's collar, breathe slowly, and remain silent. When the puppy stops barking, wait until you feel his body relax. Then, release

"Buddy up" and quietly hold the puppy's collar.

your hold on the collar. If he starts barking again, hold onto his collar. Repeat as often as necessary. The buddy system gives the puppy time to recognize you as leader, not him. It permits the puppy to make a different choice. You will be amazed by how easily behavior changes when you act as leader and use the buddy system.

Charlene's blue heeler puppy, Galahad, attacks the pooper scooper and rake. Galahad barks wildly when Charlene cleans the backyard every day. The first time Charlene uses the buddy system with Galahad, she thinks, "Can changing Galahad's behavior really be this easy?" After twenty seconds in the buddy-up position, Charlene releases her hand from his collar. Galahad stands quietly. Charlene picks up the pooper scooper. Galahad watches her, but does not bark. After two days of practicing the buddy system with Galahad, his behavior improves 90 percent. Now he rarely attacks the rake. Occasionally, when Galahad lunges at the rake, he pulls back quickly as if to say "Oops, I forgot."

Practice #4. Reinforce behavior.

Dogs notice the tiniest of details: drooping shoulders, a crooked smile, or an untied shoelace. Nothing escapes their attention, especially food. Most dogs love food. To guide a puppy's behavior, silent trainers use food, toys, or balls to reinforce a puppy's correct decisions.

Despite the best intentions, we often send puppies the wrong message. After a tough day at work, we come home and the puppy runs to see us. The puppy does not complain about a cost overrun in the budget, berate us for not filling the car with gasoline, or ask us to pick up the dry cleaning. We call a puppy's name, rub his tummy, and play fetch with his toys. We greet the puppy. We play with him and dance to his tune. Unfortunately, when we do not act like a leader, the puppy assumes he is "first dog."

Silent training allows you to show dogs their place in the pack. When puppies defer to you, you know they respect you as leader. Knowing their place in the pack creates happier and more willing puppies.

Lily sought my help with YoYo, a dominant, 11-month-old rat terrier who had issues with other dogs, people, and occasionally, Lily herself. She e-mailed me her weekly journal entries concerning the introduction of silent training to YoYo, his progress, and her concerns. The following excerpts from her e-mails show how one person applied the ideas of silent training to her dog. They offer an opportunity to see how silent training works in a real-life situation. The names and some minor details have been changed.

LILY'S JOURNAL ENTRIES CONCERNING
SILENT TRAINING AND YOYO.

February 12. My first meeting with Krista. We covered:
Crating YoYo: After opening the crate door, do not look at YoYo.

Do not establish eye contact. Do not talk. Do not touch him. Wait for YoYo to lie down of his own free will for three consecutive minutes. YoYo may exhibit a variety of behaviors to get my attention before he lies down. Ignore him. Return phone calls, read mail, or read a magazine. After he has been lying down for three minutes, call him by name and reward him with a treat.

YoYo is adjusting to being ignored when he is uncrated. It seems to take only a minute for him to lie down when he is alone with me if I sit at the table. If I am washing dishes or ironing clothes, YoYo has a harder time settling down. The greatest test is when we have guests and I ask them to ignore YoYo. It takes him longer to lie down for the required three minutes.

February 24. YoYo is no longer allowed on the furniture or in bed with us to snuggle for a while at night or in the mornings. This has been the most stressful test for him. YoYo has only tried to jump into the bed after the first two times he was told "no." He will sit and stare at us in the bed, especially if both my husband and I are in it. He paces from one side of the bed to the other. He has only jumped on a chair once. He has jumped on my husband's lap several times. YoYo now seems to understand that these places, including the bed, are off-limits.

This morning he came to my side of the bed and immediately went into a down position and stayed there for three minutes. I rewarded him and gave him attention.

One thing has become quite evident: he now sits to be petted. Before, YoYo used to immediately lie down and roll over, *demanding* a belly rub. When he does demand a belly rub, I simply stop touching him until he sits again.

Overall, his demeanor is much more relaxed.

YoYo also checks in with me much more often when he is walking on-leash. He does not try to pull as much.

Yesterday he saw a cat while walking on-leash. I simply did the gentle collar hold [buddy-up technique]. It took about thirty-five to forty seconds for his body to relax. Then he simply turned in the opposite direction and started sniffing for a good place to take care of his business.

He no longer growls when I sit by any of his beds and pet him. Now he just snuggles up for more contact.

February 26. Phase two of silent training. It is no longer required that I sit when doing silent training after uncrating him. Now, I go about routine tasks. The key is to not establish eye contact. He must realize that the leader can do anything. He must still lie down for approximately three minutes. However, we are not as stringent on having YoYo lie down for exactly three minutes.

March 10. YoYo is still ignored until he lies down for three minutes after he is uncrated. We no longer sit, but go about our household routines. He pretty much understands the program and almost immediately seeks out his bed in the closest room and lies down for three minutes. He is very happy when praised and rewarded with a treat, attention, or affection. There are moments when he relapses into old behavior, such as this morning when my husband opened his crate. I was sitting up in bed, and YoYo charged up to the bed and leapt on it. I simply pointed to the floor. He immediately got off the bed and went to his bed.

We think that one of the most obvious changes in YoYo's behavior since silent training is that he now sits to be petted. He used to immediately lie down and roll over for a belly rub. (Definitely dominant behavior in his case, as that is what he enjoyed most and demanded of anyone who touched him.) Now he sits for visitors and allows them to pet him after his required three minutes.

I am trying to take him for a walk through the neighborhood three times a week. During these walks he is not allowed to eliminate, as we do that before leaving. He is not allowed to mark or sniff the ground. He must heel and keep up with my pace. He must stop when I stop at any intersection. His fun walks occur out in the empty field next door. He has been extremely good and does not pull or become distracted by dogs barking in the yards we pass.

March 12. It is incredible that without words you can obtain leadership and control over your dog. It is a test in patience and persistence for the handler. I am learning that I must be just as persistent as my dog so that he understands that I am the leader.

When Lily assumed the role as "leader of the pack," YoYo's listening increased, his aggressive behaviors decreased, his sociability with other dogs improved, and he and Lily had more fun together. Silent trainers allow tao to direct their efforts. Leaders who follow the way of the pack move with nature, work indirectly, practice silence, and find peace. Silent trainers are kind. They have authority but use it carefully. They respect a puppy's inner nature and lead without blocking the way.

Chapter 16
Rewards: Exact Moments in Now

Tristan loves her eighteen-week-old Jack Russell terrier, Shiloh. In the morning Shiloh stands outside of Tristan's shower. As soon as she turns on the water, he dashes into the shower stall and bites at the spray. He races downstairs and through bedrooms. In the evening Shiloh runs around her swimming pool and "cannonballs" into it. In ten short weeks Shiloh steals Tristan's heart. They play ball, chase wild rabbits out of the garden, and sit together on the back porch.

Tristan thinks Shiloh should come when she calls him, lie at her feet while she watches television, greet strangers quietly, and only chew his toys. However, Shiloh has other ideas. He barks at her friends, chews her CDs, and drags pillows out the doggy door into the backyard. Tristan has confused her affection for Shiloh with training. She thinks Shiloh should do what she wants because she loves him. Instead, Tristan must design schooling sessions so Shiloh can learn self-control.

Puppies fly on automatic pilot unless we teach them differently. They chase squirrels, run after cars, and bark at the UPS driver when their instincts fire up. In order for dogs to live in a human environment, they must practice self-control. Silent trainers understand a dog's inner nature and respect it. They work with canine drives and instincts and follow the natural order. Silent trainers use rewards or "exact moments in now" to raise puppies that are *intensely motivated,* not deeply driven. As a result, puppies learn new ways to think, act, and respond.

The Tao of heaven is like the bending of a bow.

The high is lowered, and the low is raised.

If the string is too long, it is shortened;

If there is not enough, it is made longer.[17]

Drives and motivation are two ends of the same bow. Silent trainers decrease a puppy's instinctual response and increase his self-control. However, in order for puppies to learn self-control, they must connect the dots between how they act and what happens next. Silent trainers help puppies link ideas, behaviors, and consequences together. They use rewards to reinforce desirable behavior. A reinforcement is an "exact moment in now." It happens at the same time a particular behavior occurs. For example, the instant a puppy raises his right front paw to "high five," he receives a reward. In the process of learning how to "high five," a puppy discovers that what he does affects what happens next.

Silent trainers use rewards to motivate puppies to learn how to sit quietly for petting, ignore cats, and greet guests without barking. They know correctly timed food, toys, and balls increase a puppy's desire to repeat a particular action, movement, or sequence.

Puppies love to eat! However, in the pack, the leader controls food. Silent trainers respect the natural order and use food rewards in puppy schooling sessions to motivate and reward puppy performance.

The key to using food as a reward is to find a high-value food treat the puppy adores, such as hot dogs, cheese, or chicken. Cut the soft food into small, easily swallowed pieces. Do not use dry dog kibble or biscuits as rewards. Hard treats often stick in a puppy's throat since dogs frequently inhale their food without chewing. Use a puppy's hunger to your advantage. Plan schooling sessions before mealtime when a puppy's tummy is empty and needs to be filled.

A click/treat identifies, marks, and rewards.

To mark the precise moment a puppy performs a desirable action, I use a "clicker" paired with a treat, commonly abbreviated as "C/T." A clicker's unique sound helps puppies distinguish it from other noises. The most common clickers are rectangular plastic boxes that contain a metal strip inside them. When your thumb presses against the strip, it creates a distinct twanging noise. "Clicks" are neutral informational sound bites. Puppies must learn that a "click" indicates approval of a specific action, and that a reward is on its way.

A click marks the exact instant an action occurs. It means "pay attention to the behavior that earned a food reward." When puppies hear a click, they orient to you for a treat. However, a click only reinforces behavior if food immediately follows the click. Never click and then search ten seconds for a treat. Store treats in a baggie inside your pocket, wear a fanny pack, or fasten a treat bag on your belt. Then you can find a food reward quickly and give it to the puppy. Click/treat does not mean the schooling session ends. Instead, a particular action has been identified and marked. The next moment in time contains new possibilities for reinforcement. Click/treat to introduce, establish, and stabilize behaviors.

Although words are also sounds, I use C/T to accurately pinpoint the precise moment an ear flicks, paw lifts, or head lowers. I do not want to confuse a puppy with a poor ball toss, delay in squeaking a toy, prolonged enunciation of words, or slow search for a piece of cheese. By the time I finish saying "good dog," the puppy drops from a "sit" to a "down." Did the words "good dog" reward the "sit" or "down"? "Good dog" takes at least two seconds to say. Some people take more than three seconds as they linger over the vowels in "goo-ood," pause, and then say "daawg." In three seconds, puppies can sit, lie down, and roll over.

How to Turn a "Click" into an Exact Moment in Now Reward

In a quiet practice area, "click" and immediately give the puppy a small piece of chicken, cheese, hot dog, or soft treat. At this time you are not marking a specific behavior. Instead, you are teaching a puppy to associate a "click" with food. Most puppies learn the meaning of C/T after ten to twenty repetitions. When a puppy understands the meaning of "click," ears prick up, she stops what she's doing, looks at you, and expects a reward.

If the click noise scares the puppy, hide the clicker in your pocket to muffle its sound. Search for a clicker that makes a softer click, or buy a clicker where you regulate the intensity of the sound. Pip, my rescue border collie, is extremely noise-sensitive. At first, the click sound frightened her. As soon as I saw Pip's reaction, I searched for a clicker that made a softer noise. The next time I worked with Pip, I placed the clicker inside my jacket pocket to further muffle its sound. When Pip was comfortable with pocket clicks, I removed the clicker from my pocket. After a few months passed, I exchanged the quiet clicker for a loud clicker. By this time Pip knew that click meant "pay attention to the particular action you performed that earned a click and treat." Clicks no longer scare Pip; now she wants to hear them.

An "exact moment in now" informs dogs they made a correct choice. To use C/Ts effectively, plan ahead. Before any schooling session begins, decide how a finished behavior should appear. Be specific. Does name recognition mean a puppy hears her name and *looks* at you, or a puppy hears her name and *comes* to you? After you decide what the finished behavior should look like, break it into smaller teaching segments.

Figuring out the different pieces that make up a behavior sounds complicated, but it's not. Analyzing behavior is fun. It allows you to look at behavior and learning in a new way. In the same way parts of a puzzle fit together to make a picture, small simple actions form a finished behavior. During your schooling session, you start with a small response and build on it until the puppy performs the finished behavior.

How to Shape Behavior

Shaping is the art of growing behavior in small steps. You build on one action to get another response. Specific responses are identified and rewarded until the finished behavior is achieved. A puppy's first response is usually not the finished behavior. To shape a finished behavior usually requires a number of schooling sessions.

Note: The difference between luring and shaping is that luring entices dogs to perform a specific behavior by using a ball, toy, piece of chicken, or a target stick to guide the dog into a certain position. Shaping takes a behavior that a puppy offers and builds on it until the finished behavior naturally appears.

If a puppy looks confused, freezes, trembles, quits trying, or the behavior falls apart during a schooling session, stop. The puppy does not understand what you want. You are moving too fast, requiring too big a step, or trying to work on more than one aspect of behavior at a time. Do not try for speed, accuracy, and recognition simultaneously.

Too Tired to Learn

Puppies get tired. They cannot learn, retain information, or execute a perfect "come," "rollover," or "shake" when they are mentally, physically, or emotionally weary. Know your dog! For example, where dogs carry their ears indicates their readiness to learn and work. I know that if Red Sun Rising's ears stand out sideways, Pip's prick ears fold down, or Logan's ears droop, it is time to take a break. You know your puppy feels mentally, physically, or emotionally exhausted when she forgets how to "sit" when you ask her, or she refuses to enter a crate.

Emotionally overwhelmed puppies cower, growl, hide, nip ankles, bark, refuse to eat food rewards, or stop playing with toys. Quit working with a puppy when you see significant changes in behavior, body language, posture, responsiveness, or breathing during schooling sessions. Take a break. Figure out what you did or what happened that caused the puppy to shut down. Determine if you worked too long, repeated the same behavior excessively, asked for too much too fast, did not reinforce behavior often enough, executed poor timing, used unappealing food rewards, or chose a stressful location.

When you figure out why a puppy quits learning, then you can avoid it happening again. If you cannot discover why the puppy stopped trying, ask a friend, family member, or dog instructor to help you. Do not ignore it. The following signs and symptoms indicate that something is amiss. When you see body language, posture, breathing, or behavior changes, figure out how to modify the lesson, your teaching, or the situation so the puppy stays eager, motivated, and happy.

Thirteen Signs and Symptoms of Tiredness

1. Changes gait or tempo. The puppy runs faster. Spontaneous bursts of wild running. Running turns into trotting. Walking, trotting, or running slows down. The puppy stops moving or lies down. Frantic darting, spinning, jumping, leaping, or playing.

2. Alters posture. An extended or upright tail drops. Tail tucks between the back legs. The puppy's body and/or head carriage lowers, or the body tenses.

3. Changes breathing. The puppy starts panting, gulps air, hiccups, or yawns.

4. Barking increases. Bark changes in pitch.

5. Ignores you, the click, food, toys, or balls. Leaves to explore other areas.

6. Scratches frequently. The puppy stops moving, scratches, and shakes his entire body.

7. Sniffs the ground.

8. Lifts a front paw.

9. Averts eyes. Looks away, blinks, or eyes shift back and forth. Dull or glazed eyes.

10. Drooping, flickering, or flat ears.

11. Licks lips.

12. Enthusiasm and eagerness disappear. Responds slowly.

13. Stops trying. Refuses to repeat an action. Does not offer any new behaviors.

When learning ceases, take a break. Determine what caused the puppy's confusion or distress. Then you can prevent it from happening in the next schooling session. However, after a puppy successfully executes an action 10 out of 10 times, move to the next step.

How to Use a Click/Treat to Teach Name Recognition

Step 1. Decide what name recognition means to you.

In our house name recognition means a puppy identifies a word such as "Vixen" with herself. "Vixen" does not mean "come," "sit," or "stop doing that now." Name recognition asks a puppy to "Pay attention. This concerns you."

Step 2. Divide name recognition into appropriate learning segments.

Determine possible physical reactions that indicate Vixen hears and recognizes her name, such as eye contact, pricked ears, raised head carriage, a head that turns in your direction, movement toward you, or her appearance at your side.

Step 3. Find a quiet area and begin the puppy's schooling session. To review how to turn a "click/treat" into an exact moment in now reward, turn to page 162.

First, say the puppy's name in a happy voice: "Vixen."

Second, watch her body language. Does Vixen cock an ear, turn her head, or run to you? If Vixen sits quietly but lifts one ear, C/T the raised ear. If Vixen turns her head, C/T as she moves her head. If Vixen runs to you at the sound of her name, C/T as soon as she responds. Do not click when Vixen arrives at your feet. *Click/treat the exact moment you see Vixen react to hearing her name.* If you C/T after Vixen arrives at your feet, you reinforce the "come" but not the recognition of her name.

Third, first efforts deserve to be rewarded. Start with any appropriate action that Vixen offers and reinforce it. After Vixen successfully executes her first response 10 out of 10 times, withhold the click/treat until Vixen offers an improved version of the behavior. For example, instead of Vixen lifting her ears at the sound of her name, she turns her head and looks at you.

How Behavior Changes and Improves with a Click/Treat

Shaping allows you to create more sharply defined behaviors, one "click" at a time. However, the next behavior you reinforce depends on the previous behavior the puppy offers. As a silent trainer, you guide a puppy's natural reactions by using C/Ts until he performs a desired action.

You cannot rush the learning process. Puppies must understand that how they act affects what happens next. However, when you build on behaviors that a puppy volunteers, you increase a puppy's awareness and confidence step by step.

Remember, it usually takes more than one session for a puppy to demonstrate a finished behavior. If a puppy's response surpasses your wildest expectations, great. However, do not skip any steps. Wait until the puppy successfully performs a behavior 10 out of 10 times before you advance to your next step in the learning sequence, or ask for more. For example, in the beginning, I am happy if a puppy "sits." However, a puppy's first efforts are often "sloppy sits." In a sloppy sit one hip tilts to the side, the back curves, or the front paws make a crooked, rather than straight line. After a puppy demonstrates she knows the meaning of "sit" by sitting when I say "sit" 10 out of 10 times, I do not C/T if the sit is sloppy. Instead, I raise my criteria and ask for an improved version of "sit."

By this time in the schooling process, the puppy knows she earns a C/T by changing how she moves. Suddenly, she sits with a straighter back or changes the position of her front paws. I C/T at the first positive shift in her behavior. I look for small changes. If I raise my criteria too high, a puppy quits trying.

Raising criteria requires careful thinking on your part. If you raise it in too big a step, the puppy cannot meet the new standard. If the puppy does not respond or makes three incorrect choices in a row, stop the schooling session. You need to rethink and readjust your new criteria. Remember, if you increase your distance from the puppy, or ask the puppy to perform a behavior for a longer amount of time, that also raises criteria. Never increase distance and duration simultaneously; only work with one aspect of behavior at a time.

Introduce, modify, and confirm behaviors with a C/T. However, it's your relationship with a puppy that makes any reward work. "Exact moments in now" allow you to close the gap between puppies and people by communicating what you think, not in words or feelings, but by sharing a common language you both understand. A "click" tells puppies they made a correct decision. A nonverbal, respectful, informational click allows you to reinforce a puppy's behavior precisely. Paired with a treat, it motivates a puppy's desire to repeat a desired behavior. Puppies learn to associate a decision with a behavior, and a consequence. They learn that how they act earns rewards. And puppies repeat behaviors that deliver dividends.

Some puppies learn fast, while other canines progress slowly. However, they all share the same need to know when they do something right. You direct the learning process. Listen to your intuition and you will know what to require, reward, and reinforce. A click reverberates through the silence. Build a bridge between you and your puppy one "click" at a time.

Chapter 17

Silent Training and the Positive No

Hadley, a twenty-eight-week-old Scottish terrier, barks when he hears letters slide through the mail slot or the doorbell rings. With a cascade of barks, Hadley stands in front of the living room window and announces passing cars, playing children, and wandering cats in the cul-de-sac. He barks at Jennifer when she talks on the telephone, takes a shower, or plays with him.

Jennifer grew up with Scotties. She knows Scotties like to bark, but Hadley's constant barking irritates her. Although she shouts, squirts his face with water, and rattles a can filled with pennies to make him stop barking, Hadley refuses to quit. In fact, he barks more, not less. Now, Hadley barks at Jennifer when she tells him "no bark."

Hadley ignores Jennifer's water squirts, can shakes, and shouts because he does not see Jennifer as leader of their pack. Before Jennifer can decrease Hadley's barking, she must establish herself as leader. Then, Jennifer can use the "buddy system" to teach Hadley to make a different choice when he sees cars passing by, Melody and Jane skipping rope, or Sammie and Steve walking their two cattle dogs in front of the house.

Consequences teach puppies what happens when they make an incorrect choice. The buddy system is a "positive no" based on natural canine behavior. It enables puppies to make a connection between how they act and what happens next. The buddy system informs puppies when they make a bad decision and encourages them to make a different choice.

The buddy system does not add energy or create conflicts. Instead, it neutralizes the power of a situation. The consequence of adopting a leadership position by bending over, breathing slowly, and silently holding a puppy's collar until a puppy sighs, relaxes, and stops barking is that behavior changes. Puppies quit barking, digging, chewing, chasing, licking, or spinning. They accept your leadership and defer to your wishes. The buddy system solves behavior problems without punishment.

Punishment happens after the fact. Roxy runs upstairs to help her son with a math problem. Ten minutes later she walks downstairs and finds the broccoli, mushrooms, green pepper, and peapods that she left sitting on the kitchen counter in half-eaten chunks on the kitchen floor. Roxy screams at Xerxes, their twenty-six-week-old Gordon setter. *"Bad dog!* Now I can't make stir-fry for dinner tonight!" She throws a box of tissues at him. Xerxes dives for cover under the kitchen table. He does not understand why Roxy is angry. He pulled the vegetables from the counter during the first two minutes after Roxy left. For the past eight minutes, Xerxes has rested quietly under the kitchen counter.

Roxy did not see Xerxes pull mushrooms from the counter, but came downstairs and punished him anyway. Xerxes did not associate Roxy's yelling and screaming with grabbing vegetables off the kitchen counter. Instead, Xerxes learned that an angry Roxy hurt him.

Hitting, throwing, kicking, and other forms of violent behavior are counterproductive. They create fear, resentment, nervousness, depression, belligerence, and affect a puppy's confidence and trust in you. If you strike a puppy he might growl, snarl, cower, lick his lips, submissively urinate, or run away. Puppies often react to force by fighting against pressure. They act up more, not less.

Puppies remember if you hurt them. In your presence they quietly watch you or lie down. You think your punishment worked, but it failed. Physical force may temporarily stop an action, but it cannot shape behavior or teach puppies different ways to think and act. Instead, puppies wait until you leave. Then, the puppy runs, chases, chews, digs, barks, or grabs food off the counter.

A puppy's inner nature revolves around consequences. Thirsty dogs drink water. Hungry canines eat dinner. Hot dogs sit on cool tile floors in front of fans. The buddy system adopts a silent leadership position to clearly link behavior and consequence. Bending over and holding a puppy's collar establishes your position as leader and the puppy's lower rank. If a puppy does not wear a collar, place your hands gently around his neck. "Buddy up" with a puppy the instant an unwanted behavior starts. The puppy barks. Immediately reach for his collar and hold it.

The buddy system gives the puppy time to reevaluate his behavior. The pause reinforces your position as leader and gives the puppy the opportunity to make a different decision when you release him. After the puppy stops barking, relaxes, or sighs, release your hold. If a puppy starts barking again, buddy up. Repeat as often as necessary.

The buddy system works for barking, chewing, digging, hyperactivity, jumping, chasing, mouthing, spinning, leash grabbing, and obsessive-compulsive habits such as tail chasing. Pick one behavior to work on at a time. Then, follow through the first time, every time, with the buddy system.

The sage doesn't harm anyone, either.
When there's no harm on this side,
no harm on that,
goodness flows back and forth like water.[18]

The buddy system allows you to help without harming. The saluki returns to his handler instead of chasing a cat. A Skye terrier stops barking after three short woofs. The corgi quits licking the wall. A dachshund stops chasing his tail. The buddy system establishes a link between behavior and consequence. "Buddy up" and watch problems vanish.

Chapter 18
Before You Punish Your Puppy, Read This

By 10:00 A.M. on Sunday morning, Max, the six-month-old Shetland sheepdog, barked at four passing cars, dug two holes the size of the Grand Canyon in the backyard, and devoured the side of the newly re-covered couch in the living room. Hayley loved the couch, hated Max's barking, and was tired of refilling holes that Max dug. While Hayley filled the holes for the fourth time in one week, Max raced up, around, and over bushes, chairs, and flowerpots in the backyard.

Hayley stopped shoveling, grabbed her cell phone, and hit six. She waited impatiently for speed dial to process her call to Sheila, her best friend. Before Sheila finished saying hello, Hayley shouted, "Why is Max doing this? Does he hate me? He is so disobedient. I'm changing his name to Mad Max. He's driving me crazy. Some days I hate him!"

Your puppy abused his privileges. He chewed the heel off one of your white leather sandals, wet on the new, pale-yellow carpeting in the dining room, or destroyed your favorite family photograph album. Frustration from a hectic day at work and a forty-minute commute home through bumper-to-bumper traffic spills out when you walk through the door and see the destruction.

You are upset. However, punishment does not work. Punishment happens after the fact. A puppy does not understand what he did to cause you to yell, hit, or hurt him. All he knows is you came home and started shouting, grabbing, reaching for him, and striking.

You think Sasha looks "guilty" when you come home during your lunch break. In reality, Sasha reads your body language and hears the tone in your voice. She feels your anger and automatically reacts by sending you "calming signals." She drops her head, walks toward you in an arc, or lifts a front paw. You grab her and rub her nose in the wet spot on the bathroom rug. You think, "Sasha should know better. She wet on the rug to spite me because I locked her in the bathroom"—but you are wrong. A thirteen-week-old puppy cannot wait four hours before she eliminates. Puppies do not have physical bladder or sphincter control until they are between fourteen and sixteen weeks old. Sasha cannot wait for your lunch break to eliminate. Instead, you need to ask a friend, neighbor, or pet sitter to give Sasha bathroom breaks during the day. (Chapter 3 and Chapter 20 have additional ideas on how to deal with house-training issues.)

Puppies pull and drag, chase and pounce, and grab and bite. These are normal, natural behaviors. Puppies act according to their desires and the demands of the present situation. They do not chew, dig, urinate, chase, or destroy to make you angry. Puppies don't act out of malice. They don't want to hurt, retaliate, or offend you. They are happy, carefree, curious, and

Puppies pull and drag.

Puppies chase and pounce.

Puppies grab and bite.

impulsive. A puppy chews a television remote control because weak jaw muscles and newly emerging teeth demand a hard surface, and his current toys are too soft.

Never punish a puppy when your emotions are overflowing like water rushing through a broken dam. If you are angry, you cannot think clearly. When you are frustrated, you cannot accurately assess what action to take next. If you act rashly, yell, or hit a puppy, you make the situation worse, not better. Instead, take the puppy to a crate, kennel run, backyard, or laundry room. Then, call your best friend, walk around the block, mow the lawn, or weed the flower garden while you vent your feelings and work out your dismay. Do whatever it takes until your emotions are under control. Remember, puppies do not understand "good," "bad," "no," or "later." These concepts must be introduced, explained, taught, and adopted.

Silent trainers do not view behavior as "good" or "bad" but as "educated" or "ignorant." Your responsibility is to teach a puppy new ideas,

Puppy chewing a carpet.

behaviors, and responses, and give toys, bones, games, exercise, and work to occupy her mind and body. Otherwise, a puppy will invent her own rules, sports, toys, and workouts.

You may not want to hear this right now, but the barking, wetting, or chewing is not the puppy's fault. Your teaching is incomplete. A puppy's actions reflect your understanding of dog behavior and your ability to communicate, reinforce, educate, and guide a puppy's efforts.

Problems are nature's way of telling you a puppy does not understand what you want. In order to alter behavior, you need to think in new ways. Stop categorizing behavior in terms of "good" or "bad." Adopt a neutral, nonjudgmental approach that does not blame, but trusts in a natural order and applies it to solve problems.

When you follow tao, work with a puppy's strongest drives, not against them. A rottweiler that is weak in pack drive and strong in prey drive resists any attempts to physically force her to "sit." Respect her inner nature and work with her prey drive by teaching her to "fetch." Then use the toy to lure her into a "sit." After she sits, reward her by throwing the toy so she can fetch it.

Leaders who follow tao turn problems inside out and evaluate them from a puppy's point of view. Chance, a sixteen-week-old French bulldog, jumps on Millie's husband, William, when he comes home from work. Chance jumps on Millie's friends, neighborhood children, and the meter reader. Millie thinks jumping is the problem, but it's not. The real issue is Chance has not learned how to greet people. Chance jumps on William because he has not learned to sit when he sees William. When puppies do not know what you want, they improvise. However, if Millie teaches Chance to sit for petting, he will not jump on people.

Your answers to four questions will help you get to the root of any puppy performance issue. They will help you understand what to change, eliminate, simplify, and teach in order to clearly communicate to the puppy that digging holes in the garden, dragging place mats off the table, or howling at garbage trucks is unacceptable. Before you decide you have a "bad" dog, ask yourself:

1. Is my request or expectation reasonable?

2. Does the puppy know what I want?

3. Can the puppy successfully perform the desirable behavior at any time, in any place, with distractions?

4. Is the puppy getting enough physical and mental exercise?

1. Is my request or expectation reasonable?

First, you must decide if the puppy has the physical and mental maturity to do what you want. A puppy's age, personality, sex, yin or yang qualities, and the amount of time you have worked with the puppy determine if your expectations are fair. Bored, frustrated, high-energy, or anxious puppies destroy table legs, doors, or your son's plastic trucks if you do not provide appropriate toys, bones, and exercise. No one wants a puddle or pile on their floor, but is it reasonable to expect a ten-week-old puppy to exhibit bladder control? No. In this case, you need to change your expectation. However, if a dog is thirty-two weeks old, it is quite fair to expect no tinkles on the tile.

2. Does the puppy know what I want?

Puppies act according to what they know. If Alice, a seventeen-week-old Maltese, chews your daughter's gym socks, you must teach her the difference between her woolly toys and your daughter's socks. If you want Alice to "come," but do not reward her until she sits in front of you, Alice associates the reward with "sit" and not "come." Your responsibility is to design schooling sessions that clearly and precisely teach puppies what you want.

Before you blame Winston, a twenty-two-week-old pit bull, for not acting properly, you must determine if he has learned to associate a behavior with a word signal. Ask Winston to "sit," "down," "come," "roll over," or "shake." If Winston sits when you say "down," remains standing after you say "sit," or does not "come" until you repeat "come" four more times, Winston has not learned how to "down," "sit," or "come." If Winston cannot instantly perform a behavior on your first request, in any location, at any time, during any condition, he has not successfully linked a behavior with your word signal. Winston needs more schooling sessions in order to learn what you want. Chapter 20 explains how to teach "sit," "down," and "come."

Learning is a process that takes time. Disobedience is not the problem—ignorance is the real issue. Educated puppies know what people want and eagerly work with them to deliver the desired behavior.

3. Can the puppy successfully perform the desirable behavior at any time, in any place, with distractions?

Children, bicycles, shopping carts, cars, squirrels, dogs, cats, or rabbits compete for a puppy's attention. Although a puppy walks nicely on-leash at home, it does not mean she can walk quietly on-leash at the park or in a pet store. Puppies do not generalize. They must be introduced to other people, places, and things. In the same way your attention shifts from selecting the tiniest asparagus bunch to staring at a clown who suddenly juggles three broccoli bunches in a grocery store aisle, a puppy twists, turns, and focuses her attention when three members of the high school track team run past you at the park. However, if you work with a puppy in new locations and around family members, strangers, cars, and bicycles, the puppy learns that it doesn't matter where, when, why, or how you ask, she will listen to you and follow your instructions.

When a puppy can successfully perform a behavior 10 out of 10 times, thirty days in a row, in the house, at the park, in front of neighbors and running children, you can trust that the puppy knows the behavior.

4. Is the puppy getting enough physical and mental exercise?

Draw a large circle on a piece of paper. Divide it into twenty-four equal parts. Take a blue pen and color the hours the puppy sleeps. Use a red pen for eating, green pen for playing, orange pen for exercise, black pen for working with you, gold pen for time spent with other dogs, purple pen for socializing with other people, and leave white for time spent alone. Which color dominates? Most puppies need more schooling sessions, more socialization with other dogs and people, and more exercise. However, do not take your puppy for a four-mile run. Their bones cannot handle intense, sustained workouts. Instead, increase their exercise by playing games, fetching toys, catching balls, or taking short walks in the backyard or at the park. If you are too busy to work with your puppy, find someone to assist you. Dog trainers, pet walkers, neighbors, family members, and friends can help you with a new puppy.

Puppies run, chase, play, and rest.

Puppies run, chase, play, and rest. If you design exercise sessions that work a puppy's brain and her body, Chelsea, the twenty-three-week-old border terrier, will have a reason to rest and relax while you are at the grocery store. A perfect puppy workout that stimulates her mentally and challenges her physical energy is to walk her on-leash in the backyard for five minutes. During the walk, ask the puppy to do something different every twenty or thirty seconds, such as sit, down, turn right, turn left, circle right, circle left, walk ten steps, or run fifteen steps. After five minutes of following your directions, a puppy's mind gets tired. A weary brain creates a relaxed body that wants to rest.

At 7:00 P.M. on Saturday night, you have a dinner date. At 6:45 P.M. it's time to take the puppy out for one last bathroom break. As you walk along the path to the backyard, the sprinkler system starts. Three jets of water spray your French silk shirt, strike your face, and hit your jeans. With cold water dripping from your hands, you know the puppy has demolished the sprinkler system again. Yelling and shouting, you race to the edge of the yard. Suddenly, you're in a free fall. The puppy has pushed you over the edge. There's no one to catch you, so you have to catch yourself. Remember:

> *Love is stronger than anger,*
> *silence more profound than wild words, or*
> *sharp slaps.*
> *Anchor your actions in tao,*
> *act in harmony, and*
> *catch yourself.*
> *Success comes by solving problems from within,*
> *when you know why puppies eat sprinkler systems,*
> *you won't need discipline.*

Understand a puppy's needs,
adopt them as your own, and
lead with loving kindness.

Silent trainers are not people without any puppy problems. They are successful pack leaders who learn to solve problems by following tao. Allow tao to guide your efforts. Then you will understand the relationship between a puppy's age and chewing, amount of exercise and destruction, confinement and hyperactivity, curiosity and boredom, and where the true responsibility for a puppy's behavior lies. I'll give you a hint: Do not blame the puppy.

Part 4 | The Way of Practice

Chapter 19
Five Practices to Grow
Good Puppy Behavior

"Ouch! That hurts. Don't bite my fingers; take the food treat in my hand." How do you teach a hungry, eager puppy to gently take a food reward and not bite your fingers? Silent training helps you follow the natural order of events and with a minimum amount of effort, raise a good dog. By following tao you understand behavior at its roots. And the roots of tao are yin and yang.

Yin and yang define, complement, and alternate with each other: cold/hot, wet/dry, up/down, in/out, and fast/slow. When you add water to dry, hard yang kibble to soften it for tender puppy gums, it turns into

Playing is yang.

Resting is yin.

moist, easily chewed, yin kibble. A puppy who runs next to you while you jog demonstrates yang. However, when you stop and stand still to catch your breath, and the puppy sits at your feet, that's yin. During on-leash work you fine-tune the balance between yin and yang when you change from walk to run, sit, walk, sit, and run again. Active, assertive, interactive behavior is yang. Quiet, passive actions are yin. To walk forward is yang; to stay is yin.

All canine behavior represents different aspects and interactions between yin and yang. Silent trainers adjust, change, and interact to maintain the balance and create a healthy, friendly, well-mannered puppy. They do not use force. Coercion destroys balance because it does not allow yin and yang to alter, adapt, and evolve. Instead, silent trainers use behavior-contingent rewards to build puppy confidence, awareness, and trust.

Those who wish to use Tao to influence others
don't rely on force or weapons or
military strategies.
Force rebounds.
Weapons turn on their wielders.
Battles are inevitably followed by famines.
Just do what needs to be done, and then stop.[19]

Before you can help a puppy link ideas, behaviors, and rewards together, you must decide what a puppy must learn to live happily with you. The following five practices can help you grow good puppy behavior and design effective teaching situations.

Practice 1. Observe the puppy to discover whether the puppy shows a majority of yin or yang characteristics.

Practice 2. Determine the characteristics of the "finished" behavior.

Practice 3. Divide a finished behavior into smaller teaching segments.

Practice 4. Teach, practice, and maintain behavior.

Practice 5. "Proof" the behavior.

Practice 1. Observe the puppy to discover whether the puppy shows a majority of yin or yang characteristics.

A puppy's ability to respond to your requests is influenced by her yin (quiet, mellow) or yang (noisy, active) attitude. Yin puppies easily learn how to "sit." However, they may have a harder time learning how to "fetch." Yang puppies enjoy coming to you, but they may have a more difficult time learning how to "stay." Understanding the nature of your puppy helps you design learning situations that work to the puppy's advantage.

Practice 2. **Before you start a schooling session, determine the characteristics of the "finished" behavior.**

Does "roll over" mean a puppy rolls on his back from right-side to left-side, or does "roll over" signify that a puppy rolls over from right-side to left-side to right-side? Before you start a schooling session, decide how the finished behavior appears. Then, you will know what actions to reward and you can prevent any confusion between you and the puppy.

Practice 3. **Divide a finished behavior into smaller teaching segments.**

Determine the components of the behavior you want to teach. For example, if you want to teach a puppy to "wave," the puppy must learn to raise a front paw, and move it up and down. Now divide it into smaller learning segments. Think about the possible responses a puppy might offer that you can reward. For example, the puppy lifts a paw. The puppy raises a front paw one inch above the ground. The puppy raises the front paw two to three inches above the ground. The puppy raises her paw to her chest. The puppy lifts her paw to nose level. The puppy moves the paw up and down by her muzzle. To grow behavior, each step must build on the previous step. Never proceed to the next step until the previous step has been mastered.

One of the first lessons I teach puppies is to find a target lying on the ground. A target can be a Frisbee, a lid to a plastic container, or a computer mouse pad. Targets help me teach puppies to run through a doggy door, go to a crate, lie on a specific rug, run through an agility tunnel, and learn that words are signals.

The finished behavior of finding a target consists of a puppy standing at a target, looking at it, and waiting. To teach targeting, the behavior

Find the target.

is divided into the following segments: the puppy looks at a target, moves toward it, reaches it, and waits at the target. Depending on the puppy, additional steps may be added or subtracted. During schooling sessions, a

C/T reinforces a puppy when she looks, moves toward, reaches, stops, stares, and finally, waits at the target.

Step-by-Step:

How to Teach Targeting

To teach a dog to find a target, bring the puppy to a quiet room, close the door, and place the target on the floor. Puppies are curious. Even the shyest puppy looks at a new object on the floor.

Start with any appropriate behavior the puppy offers that indicates the puppy has seen the target, and then C/T. At this point, the puppy does not know what you want. Wait to see what the puppy does. She might stare at the target, walk over to it, bark, stand above the target, or grab it with her mouth. The possibilities are endless. Bold, adventurous, yang puppies inspect targets immediately. They might nose the target, bark, or grab it with their mouth. Shy, timid, yin puppies might look or back away. Start with any positive behavior that the puppy offers and shape it into a finished behavior.

Remember, every puppy learns at a different rate. Plus, puppies have short attention spans. Any time you teach new behaviors, take breaks during each schooling session so the puppy stays eager to learn. Keep your puppy's attitude fresh with ten-second, thirty-second, or one-minute schooling sessions.

After each step in the following learning sequence, remove the target after the C/T. Then, replace the target before you repeat the step or ask for the next step.

IMPORTANT! Do not advance to the next step until the puppy has mastered the current step! Most steps need between five to ten repetitions before you can progress to the next step.

Step 1. Place the target two feet in front of Rascal.

Step 2. Rascal turns his head and looks at the target; C/T.

Step 3. Rascal walks toward the target; C/T.

Step 4. He reaches the target; C/T.

Step 5. Rascal lowers his head; C/T.

Step 6. Rascal stares at the target; C/T.

Step 7. After a puppy consistently performs a finished behavior, it's time to add a word signal. When Rascal successfully finds, stands above the target, and stares at it ten out of ten times, it's time to associate the word signal "get it" with the finished behavior of seeing a target, moving to it, standing above it, and staring.

Step 8. Start by saying "get it," *just before* Rascal reaches the target, stands above it, stares, and earns his C/T.

> *Note: Only say "get it" once. Otherwise, Rascal might think the signal is "get it, get it, get it."*

Step 9. Replace the target on the floor. Do not wait until Rascal almost reaches the target before saying "get it." Instead, say "get it" immediately. C/T after he reaches the target, stands above it, and stares.

Step 10. After you place the target on the floor for the eleventh time, do not say "get it." Remain silent. If the puppy finds, stands, and stares at the target, do not C/T, talk, or touch the puppy. You have not given the puppy the word signal "get it." This step teaches puppies they must listen for a word signal *before* performing a behavior.

Step 11. Pick up the target.

Step 12. Replace the target and say "get it."

Step 13. When Rascal reaches the target, stands above it, and stares, C/T.

Step 14. Repeat steps 8, 9, 10, 11, 12, and 13 until the puppy does not move when you place the target on the floor, but waits for you to say "get it" before he goes to the target. A puppy's ability to wait for a word signal before he acts demonstrates that he understands the relationship between words and behavior. This process will take more than one schooling session. Do not expect finished behaviors in one lesson.

Step 15. Increase the target's distance from Rascal by two more feet. Say "get it." When Rascal finds, stands, and stares at the target, C/T.

Step 16. Continue to increase distance in two- to three-foot increments until Rascal can locate a target twenty feet away.

If a Puppy Cannot Figure Out the Next Step

At any time during an exercise, if a puppy cannot perform the next step after three attempts, stop. You have asked for too big a step. Reevaluate and readjust. Figure out a smaller step that the puppy will understand. Then, return to the previous step. After the puppy successfully masters the previous step, add the new smaller step.

Puppies Who Skip Steps

Some puppies skip steps. They might see the tray and immediately run to it. Great! However, you still need to shape them standing at the target, staring, and waiting. Fast learners and thinkers require that you know the finished behavior in case they move ahead quickly.

Note: You do not have to use a clicker to teach behavior performance pairs. Instead, "cluck" with your tongue, say "yup," " 'kay," or use any single-word or single-tone combination. Avoid two-syllable words. For example, " 'kay" is quicker to say than "okay"; "x" is better than "excellent." Hard consonants at the end of a word prevent you from drawing out the word, such as "yup" instead of "yes-s-s." Remember to use the same word and tone of voice every time when you identify a particular action.

Practice 4. Teach, practice, and maintain behavior.

Plan at least one, short, five-minute or less "official" schooling session once a day. If your schedule permits it, include additional five-minute sessions. They are easy to fit in before you leave for work, after you arrive home, or in the evening. Incorporate other mini-schooling sessions while you watch television, wash dishes, fold laundry, or brush your teeth. For example, a one-half-hour television program usually has three commercial breaks; three perfect opportunities to school the puppy in "sit," "down," "roll over," or "high five."

After a puppy learns a new behavior, you can ask for more. To improve a behavior's duration, distance, speed, accuracy, or intensity requires that you withhold the click/treat until the puppy offers a better version of the behavior.

To increase a puppy's ability to perform a behavior for a longer period of time, delay the time between the behavior and the C/T. For example, when a puppy "comes," you do not want the puppy to run to you and then immediately zoom off. *Build duration by delaying the time between when the puppy arrives at your feet and the C/T.* When the puppy first comes and stands near you, wait to reward him until two seconds pass. The next time the puppy arrives at your feet, wait four seconds before you C/T. The following time, hold off until six seconds pass. Then, surprise him. Reward him at two seconds again. Keep the puppy focused on you and his behavior by varying when he earns a reward. Slowly build up the time you expect the puppy to remain near you. At the next session, reward the puppy at three seconds, six seconds, two seconds, then eight seconds. Each session builds on the previous session. After a puppy remains near you for the desired amount of time, release him with a "free" signal.

Note: Do not school for two aspects of behavior at the same time, such as greater distance and increased duration, or faster speed and extreme accuracy. Instead, concentrate on one aspect at a time. For example, first increase the amount of time that a puppy sit-stays. After the puppy successfully sit-stays for the desired length of time with you standing next to her, in future schooling sessions, slowly increase your distance from the puppy.

The process for improving behavior is always the same. Work with an initial response and allow the behavior to unfold naturally. After the puppy performs a complete behavior, determine if any aspect of the behavior needs improvement, such as speed, accuracy, intensity, time, or distance to create a polished performance. Then, choose one aspect and design schooling sessions to build it.

Practice 5. "Proof" the behavior.
Proofing requires that you practice with a puppy in other locations with a variety of distractions. In the beginning, hold schooling sessions in a quiet area inside the house, garage, or basement that is free of distractions. When the puppy successfully performs a behavior ten out of ten times in one location and associates a word signal with the behavior, increase the number and type of distractions in the practice area. Build to exciting, challenging, high-level distractions slowly.

Start with stationary, boring, non-interesting distractions such as car keys, a shoebox, a paper bag, or a towel. Then, replace those distractions with an old toy, dog food dish, or a tree branch. Next, add interesting, motionless items, such as food, a dog dish filled with kibble, a favorite toy, or a person sitting quietly.

Increase the interest-level of the distraction. More difficult distractions for puppies to ignore are movements, sounds, and other animals, such as when you make lunch or wash dishes; adults walking through a room; children playing games with a ball; children running; ringing of the doorbell; a visitor opening the front door; someone walking up to talk to you; a person reaching down to pet the puppy; another dog walking, running, or playing; cats sleeping or eating; squirrels running across the grass; or birds chirping.

Gradually increase the number and appeal of distractions while you school the dog. Initially, you can turn on a television or radio while you practice. Then, ask your wife, brother, or friend to watch you school the puppy. During future sessions, ask your sister to walk to the other side of the family room, play a song on the piano, or do sit-ups on the floor, while the puppy practices her sit-stay.

Use your imagination. Include distractions you think a puppy might encounter during a walk or visit to the veterinarian's office. Have a friend sit next to you on the couch, and ask the puppy to sit quietly at your feet. Walk a puppy on-leash during a basketball practice session in your backyard.

After puppies successfully demonstrate a behavior with distractions in one location, move to a new location. Possible schooling areas occur in the house, garage, basement, backyard, front yard, friend's backyard, park, children's playground, pet store, or local outdoor café that allows dogs. When you change to another location, the puppy's performance may drop. Re-school, practice, and soon the puppy will "sit," "down," "come," "shake," and "roll over" in the new area. Puppies demonstrate "finished" behaviors when they can perform an action at any time and in any place.

Chapter 20
Nine Performance Pairs

Behavior performance pairs follow the idea of yin and yang to introduce, solve, and maintain puppy behaviors. Performance pairs balance behavior when they oppose, alternate, and change aspects. As one feature diminishes, another feature grows. For example, yang barking decreases and yin quiet increases. The following exercises describe nine yin/yang performance pairs every puppy needs to learn: look/free, sit/down, take it/leave it, up/off, gentle/tug, bark/quiet, come/place, walk/stay, and inside/outside.

When you practice the following behaviors, find a quiet location and begin the schooling session. The puppy can be on- or off-leash. If the puppy is off-leash when he walks into a room, he may start exploring it. If you do not have time to wait for this curiosity phase to finish, use a leash with the puppy.

Each performance pair contains a description of the finished behavior according to my criteria. You may have different standards. Define a behavior according to your terms. For example, as long as the puppy "lies down," you may not care if the puppy lies on his side or if he lies so that his belly touches the ground. You must decide what the finished behavior looks like. Then, you can provide consistent guidance when you school the puppy.

Puppies must progress through many small steps to master a specific behavior. If you skip steps, puppies become confused and learning suffers. However, when puppies understand what action to perform, they learn quickly, and in a short amount of time.

Observe the puppy and use your intuition to determine the number of steps required to divide a behavior into appropriate learning segments; when to change to the next step, distraction, or location; and when to add a word signal.

The performance pair step-by-step instructions are only suggestions. Review them. Change, add, or delete steps, so that they work with your puppy's inner nature. Every step requires frequent repetitions. *Although each step is listed only once, plan on repeating a step between five to fifteen times. Wait until the puppy masters the current step before moving to the next step.* Observe the puppy's responses and follow your intuition to determine when to change to the next step, distraction, or location. Plan on several sessions, days, and/or weeks for the puppy to master a behavior.

How often a puppy repeats a step depends on the puppy's personality, the complexity of the behavior, the amount of time you work with the puppy, your skill at creating effective learning sequences, and your ability to reward the puppy at the exact instant he performs an action. After puppies successfully perform a desired action ten out of ten times, they are usually ready for the next step. Your puppy may need more or fewer repetitions. Use your imagination and stimulate the canine brain.

Performance pairs are based on the idea of yin and yang. When behaviors complement each other, puppies learn faster and more easily. Although the following behaviors are paired, they do not always have to be combined in the same session. However, combining behaviors in the same session, such as "bark" and "quiet," or "up" and "off," helps learning happen quickly with less effort.

Note: If you decide not to use a click/treat (C/T), substitute the word, sound, or signal you plan on using in the following exercises.

THE FIRST PERFORMANCE PAIR: LOOK AND FREE

"Look" requires a puppy to maintain eye contact with you for twenty seconds while her feet remain firmly planted on the ground. When puppies focus on you, they do not pay attention to joggers, remote-controlled cars, boys playing softball, or two terriers running down the street.

Puppies need to act like dogs. "Free" tells puppies a particular lesson is finished. It gives puppies permission to focus on something besides you. They are now free to explore, relax, and follow their own agenda. Puppies who know that playtime happens during and after lessons develop into happy, stress-free, well-mannered dogs.

How to Teach Look

Step 1. Look at the puppy. Stare at the top of the puppy's head. The puppy will feel your gaze and look in your direction; C/T.

Step 2. Stare at the top of the puppy's head. If the puppy's first response was to look at your knees, wait until the puppy looks further up your body (for example, your belt buckle); C/T.

Step 3. Stare at the top of the puppy's head. Wait until the puppy looks further up your body (for example, your chest); C/T.

Step 4. Stare at the top of the puppy's head. Wait until the puppy looks at your face; C/T.

Step 5. Stare at the top of the puppy's head. Wait until the puppy looks in your eyes; C/T.

Increase the amount of time between when the puppy looks at you and when she earns the C/T. Wait two seconds, three seconds, five seconds; build up to twenty seconds before you C/T.

Step 6. After the puppy watches you regularly for twenty seconds, add the word signal "look." (Turn to page 191 to review how to add a word signal to a behavior.)

Extra Help

Puppies follow sound and movement. If a puppy does not feel your stare, say her name, make a small noise, or take your finger and bring it close to her nose. If necessary, lightly tap her nose. Then, draw your finger toward your face. You are using your finger to lure her eyes to your face. Once the puppy finds your face, fade the lure by saying her name more softly, making a barely audible noise, and moving your finger less and less until it just rests by your nose. Then, add the word signal "look."

Step 7. Practice and proof. Hold a toy, food bowl, or ball that you think the puppy likes in one hand. Start with the puppy's least favorite toy and work up to her favorite toy. Say "look." When the puppy looks at you instead of the toy in your hand, C/T. Repeat. Start with stationary objects, and then add moving objects and people. Follow your intuition to determine when to add the next distraction. Change locations and repeat.

Note. Each step requires many repetitions. Observe the puppy's responses and follow your intuition to determine when to change to the next step, distraction, or location. Plan on several sessions, days, and/or weeks for the puppy to master the behavior.

How to Teach Free

Step 1. To release a puppy from focusing on you, say "free."

Note: If you are using a leash, unhook the leash from her collar.

Step 2. As the puppy leaves, praise her softly. Say "good girl" when she leaves you to sniff, roll in the grass, or inspect the flowers. After each session, release the puppy in a different way. You can scratch the puppy under the ears, on her neck, or along her sides. Or, walk away and clap your hands to encourage the puppy to run and explore.

Proofing is unnecessary with this exercise.

THE SECOND PERFORMANCE PAIR: SIT AND DOWN

"Sit" requires a puppy to fold his hind legs so they tuck under his rear end as it rests on the ground. The puppy's back and hips are straight. The front legs remain vertical, and the front paws form a straight, even line. A puppy who sits cannot run out the door or jump on people. At the veterinarian's office, a sit allows a veterinarian to inspect ears, muzzle, eyes, and mouth easily. During a trip to a crowded store, a "sit" prevents puppies from exploring shelves or visiting other people while you shop or wait in line. On a walk while you wait at a stoplight, "sit" keeps puppies safe from moving people, bicycles, and cars.

"Down" requires dogs to make complete contact with their belly on the floor or ground. Puppies that lie down cannot run out the door or jump on people. During visits to the veterinarian, lying down allows a veterinarian to feel a puppy's back, sides, tail, and hind end, or insert a thermometer into his rectum. Lying down keeps a puppy's nose from sniffing your food, visiting guests, or getting in your way while you cook dinner.

How to Teach Sit

Step 1. Dogs sit many times during a day. A natural way to teach sit is to C/T when you see the puppy sit at any time during the day. Puppies repeat behaviors that earn rewards. Soon the puppy offers a sit to earn a C/T.

Sit.

Down.

Step 2. Add the word signal "sit." (Turn to page 191 to review how to add a word signal to a behavior.)

Step 3. Practice and proof. To prepare for future veterinary visits, ask friends and family members to touch the puppy while she sits. Direct them to open her mouth, look at her teeth, and lift her ears. Change locations and repeat.

EXTRA HELP

Another way to teach sit is to use a piece of food and lure a puppy into a sit. You can combine a lure with a C/T.

Step 1. Face the puppy. In your left hand, take a piece of cheese, hot dog, or chicken and hold it approximately two inches away from the dog's face.

Step 2. Move your hand over the puppy's head, slowly toward the puppy's hind end. As the puppy tracks the movement of your hand, it will cause his hindquarters to automatically engage and lower. (If you hold the chicken too high above the puppy's head, he will jump to reach it.)

Step 3. When the puppy sits, C/T and give him the chicken.

Step 4. Add the word signal "sit"; C/T.

Step 5. Ask the puppy to "sit" without using the lure; C/T.

Step 6. Practice and proof. Incorporate "sits" into your daily routine. Puppies can sit before eating, playing, going outside, or friendly scratches. Ask the puppy to sit while you stand next to, in front of, or behind him. Ask the puppy to sit while you lie on the floor, stand with your back turned to the dog, read a magazine, or wash dishes.

To prepare the puppy for visits to the veterinarian, ask friends and family members to pet or touch the puppy while she sits. They can open her mouth, lift her ears, lift her tail, and touch her feet.

How to Teach Down

Step 1. Dogs lie down many times during a day. A natural way to teach "down" is to C/T when it happens. Puppies repeat behaviors that earn rewards. Soon the puppy lies down because he knows lying down earns a reward.

Step 2. Add the word signal "down." (Turn to page 191 to review how to add a word signal to a behavior.)

Step 3. Practice and proof. To prepare for future veterinary visits, ask friends and family members to touch the puppy while he lies down. Direct them to touch and hold his paws, run their hands down his back or on his stomach, and lift his tail. Change locations and repeat.

EXTRA HELP

Another way to teach a puppy to lie down is to take a high-value food treat and lure him into a down. You can combine a lure with a C/T.

Step 1. Face the puppy. In your hand take a piece of cheese, hot dog, or chicken and hold it approximately two inches away from the dog's face.

Step 2. Allow your hand to slowly drop to the ground between the puppy's front legs. Then, slowly draw your hand along the ground three to six inches past the front legs. It will feel like you are drawing the letter "L" with your hand. As the puppy tracks the movement of your hand, it causes his body to sink to the ground. Some puppies immediately lie down.

Note: If the puppy does not lie down right away, shape the behavior. First, C/T as the puppy sinks his head. Second, C/T while he lowers his head and neck further. Third, C/T as he drops his body. Finally, C/T when the he rests his body on the ground.

Step 3. When the puppy lies down, C/T.

Step 4. Add the word signal "down"; C/T. (Turn to page 191 to review how to add a word signal to a behavior.)

Step 5. Ask the puppy to lie down without using the lure; C/T.

Step 6. Practice and proof. Incorporate lying down into your daily routine. Puppies can lie down before eating, playing, going outside, or friendly scratches. Ask the puppy to lie down while you stand next to, in front of, or behind him. Ask him to lie down while you sit on the floor, stand with your back turned to the puppy, read a magazine, or wash dishes.

To prepare for future veterinary visits, ask friends and family members to touch the puppy while he lies down. Direct them to touch and hold his paws, run their hands down his back or on his stomach, and lift his tail. Change locations and repeat.

THE THIRD PERFORMANCE PAIR: TAKE IT AND LEAVE IT

"Take it" requires puppies to pick up a toy, piece of food, or other item with their mouth. It teaches shy yin puppies how to take a food treat from your hand and pick up a ball or toy on the floor. It gives active yang puppies a job; how to pick up their toys and place them in a toy box, or how to find the car keys you lost inside the house. "Take it" teaches assertive yang puppies you are leader because the leader controls food.

"Leave it" requires that puppies quit touching or avoid interacting with a specific object, person, or animal. It stops mouthing, chewing

Step 1. Take it.

Step 2. Take it.

Step 3 and Step 5. Leave it.

Step 4. Leave it.

Step 6. Leave it.

inappropriate items, leash grabbing, and digging. Leave it keeps puppies from sniffing snakes, picking up toads, or chasing cats and squirrels. It prevents puppies from grabbing dead birds, taking food off the table, or playing "keep-away" with your daughter's Barbie dolls.

A natural way to teach "take it" and "leave it" is to pair them together in the same session.

How to Teach Take It and Leave It

Step 1. Sit in a chair. Place a dry food treat in the palm of your hand. Keep your hand open so the puppy can see the treat. Lower your hand until it is at the same height as the puppy's muzzle. When the puppy takes the treat, C/T.

Step 2. Say "take it" *immediately before* the puppy takes the treat. Repeat at least five times.

Step 3. After you place a treat in your hand for the sixth time, do not say "take it." Remain silent. If the puppy reaches for the treat, quickly cover the treat with your fingers.

Step 4. The puppy may sniff, lick, or nose your hand. As soon as the puppy stops touching, C/T. Give him a treat from your other hand.

Step 5. Add the word signal "leave it." (Turn to page 191 to review how to add a word signal to a behavior.)

Step 6. Repeat steps 3, 4, and 5 until you can hold out a treat in your open hand, say "leave it," and the puppy does not move to take it.

Step 7. Increase the amount of time the puppy cannot touch your hand. Start with two seconds. Increase the amount of time gradually until the puppy can "leave it" for ten seconds.

Step 8. Practice and proof. Change treats from a piece of dry dog kibble to more desirable food treats, such as a dog biscuit, cheese, or chicken. When the puppy performs "take it" and "leave it" with food, change to other favorite items such as toys or balls. Next, change from holding a treat in your hand to placing it on the floor. Start with a piece of dry dog food. When you say "leave it," be prepared to grab the treat with your hand or cover it with your foot. Continue to practice with more desirable food treats and other favorite items. Then, change locations.

EXTRA HELP

If the puppy is not interested in the treat in your hand, change to a more desirable treat such as chicken, cheese, or dried liver.

If a puppy does not know how to pick up a toy, ball, or car keys with his mouth, you need to shape the behavior. First, C/T a look, then a sniff, touch, open mouth, teeth touch, teeth hold, close mouth around item, lift item in mouth, and hold item in mouth.

EXTRA HELP

If a puppy grabs your fingers or hand, turn to the "gentle/tug" behavior pair for help with this issue.

THE FOURTH PERFORMANCE PAIR: UP AND OFF

"Up" informs a puppy to leave his current location and move to the top of something. "Up" stops a puppy from planting his feet and refusing to move where you want. Say "up" when you want a dog to get in a car, jump on a scale at the veterinarian's office to be weighed, or climb into a grooming tub for bathing.

"Off" directs a puppy to remove himself from his current location. "Off" keeps puppies from jumping on people, furniture, or counters. When a puppy lies on your son's clothes that are scattered on his bedroom floor, "off" tells him to move to a different location.

A natural way to teach "up" and "off" is to pair them together in the same session.

How to Teach Up and Off

Step 1. The easiest way to teach "up" is to place a target on a low table. (Page 190 describes how to teach a puppy to find a target.) The puppy already knows a target means "find, stand, and stare at the target to earn a reward." As the puppy jumps up on the table, C/T.

Step 2. Add the word signal "up." (Turn to page 191 to review how to add a word signal to a behavior.)

Step 3. You can teach "off" in two different ways. You can wait until the puppy jumps off the table and C/T. Or, you can use your hand as a lure. Puppies follow movement. With your hand or finger, move it from the puppy's nose and point to a place on the ground. The puppy will follow your gesture and move to where you are aiming. As the puppy leaves the table, C/T.

Step 4. Add the word signal "off." (Turn to page 191 to review how to add a word signal to a behavior.)

Step 5. Practice and proof. Practice "up" and "off" with a picnic bench, open car hatch, boat seat, or children's playground equipment.

EXTRA HELP

If your puppy does not know how to find a target, you must shape the "up." For example, when the puppy looks at the table, C/T. Steps toward the table, C/T. Reaches the table, C/T. Places her head over the table, C/T. Puts front paws on the table, C/T. Places all four paws on the table, C/T. After the puppy understands that "up" means "four feet on a raised object," add the word signal "up."

EXTRA HELP

Another easy way to teach "off" is to let gravity do the work. When a puppy jumps on you, do not talk to, touch, or look at the puppy. Wait. Gravity, and a dog's body structure that causes him to walk on four legs, will return his front feet to the floor. As soon as his front feet touch the ground, C/T.

Add the word signal "off."

THE FIFTH PERFORMANCE PAIR: GENTLE AND TUG

"Gentle" means a puppy does not grab, chew, bite, chomp, mouth, or nibble your hands or fingers when you feed her a treat. Instead, a puppy gently takes a treat, toy, ball, or other items safely from your hands.

"Tug" directs puppies to hold onto a rope or toy and pull. Timid yin puppies often need to learn how to pull. "Tug" decreases fear and increases confidence and happiness. "Tug" teaches bold yang puppies to play gently. They also learn that the leader starts and stops all games. With puppies that are not attracted to food treats, "tug" can replace food as a re-

To teach "gentle," leave a dime-sized opening.

ward. In addition, puppies can "tug" and open a door, drag a buoy, or play a game. However, never allow a puppy to pull on your clothes, gloves, or other personal items.

How to Teach Gentle

Step 1. Make a loose fist with your hand. Curl your fingers next to your palm. Leave a dime-sized opening where your index finger bends. Push peanut butter or soft cheese into the opening, or any soft food that a puppy licks instead of bites.

Step 2. Hold your hand at the same height as the puppy's muzzle. When the puppy licks the peanut butter, C/T. Repeat until the puppy consistently licks, not bites, the peanut butter.

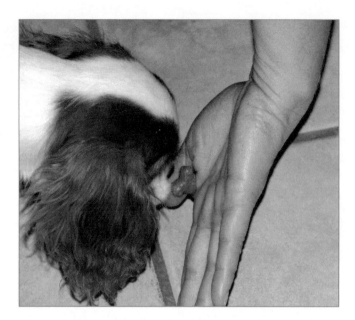

Place a hard treat in the groove between your thumb and index finger.

Step 3. Increase the amount of time between when a puppy licks and you C/T. Start with two seconds and build to six seconds.

Step 4. Add the word signal "gentle." (Turn to page 191 to review how to add a word signal to a behavior.)

Step 5. Practice and proof. Hold a piece of cheese, hot dog, or soft treat between your fingers. When the dog licks it, C/T.

Step 6. Place a small, hard dog treat in the groove between your thumb and index finger. Squeeze your thumb and index finger together to hold it in place. Let the biscuit edge stick out at least one-half inch from the palm side of your hand.

Step 7. Say "gentle"; C/T. If the puppy lunges for the biscuit, say, "leave it."

Step 8. Practice and proof. After the puppy understands how to take a food treat gently from your hands, ask other adults to practice with the puppy. When the puppy consistently takes a treat from adult hands, work with your children on this exercise.

EXTRA HELP

If a puppy bites your fingers, repeat steps 1 through 5. You have moved too fast. The puppy has not yet learned the meaning of "gentle."

How to Teach Tug

Drag and wiggle a thick rope tug toy on the ground in front of the puppy. Yang puppies instantly leap, grab, and tug. However, yin puppies need to be taught to interact with a toy. To shape this behavior, use the following steps:

Step 1. The puppy looks at the tug toy; C/T.

Step 2. Sniffs the tug toy; C/T.

Step 3. Touches the tug toy; C/T.

Step 4. Opens mouth as she touches the tug toy; C/T.

Step 5. Teeth touch the tug toy; C/T.

Step 6. Teeth grab the tug toy; C/T.

Step 7. Mouth closes around the tug toy; C/T.

Step 8. Pulls back on the tug toy; C/T.

Note: If the puppy will not tug, place one hand on her chest and gently hold the puppy in place, while your other hand tugs on the toy. When the puppy tugs, C/T.

Step 9. Add the word signal "tug." (Turn to page 191 to review how to add a word signal to a behavior.)

Step 10. At the end of tug, say "leave it." Add another phrase that means playtime is finished, such as "that's all" or "over and out." Take the toy and put it where the puppy cannot reach it. Remember, the leader starts and stops all games and controls access to toys.

Step 11. Practice and proof. First, teach "tug" inside the house. Then, play "tug" in other locations. Plan short tug sessions with yang puppies to prevent over-enthusiastic responses.

EXTRA HELP

Other toys besides ropes can be used as tug toys. However, make sure they are soft and pliable. Hard toys can damage puppy teeth and gums.

THE SIXTH PERFORMANCE PAIR: BARK AND QUIET

"Bark" directs a puppy to bark until you tell her to stop barking. Frequently, many puppies who learn how to "bark" on signal will not bark unless instructed. "Bark" also is a useful signal if you live alone. "Quiet" advises puppies to stop barking immediately. It decreases barking at doorbells, cars, strangers, guests, pedestrians, bicyclists, or any unfamiliar person or object.

A natural way to teach "bark" and "quiet" is to pair them together in the same session.

How to Teach Bark and Quiet

Step 1. What causes your puppy to bark? If the puppy barks while she waits for you to fill her dish, use this knowledge to your advantage. Get her dish, wait, and when she barks, C/T.

Step 2. Because you do not want to link the bark signal with a puppy's food dish, think of other events that cause the puppy to bark, such as bouncing a ball, ringing a bell, seeing a cat, opening the garage door, or making funny noises. Alternate what you do to elicit a puppy's barking.

EXTRA HELP

If a puppy is naturally "barky," wait until the puppy sponta-neously starts barking to begin your "bark" and "quiet" school-ing session.

Step 3. At first, you may need to interrupt the barking with a quick hand gesture, whistle, a snap of your fingers, by physically backing away, or by lightly stomping your feet. The puppy may turn his head, raise his eyebrows, or lift his ears to look at you. Click/treat the moment his mouth closes and he stops barking. You want him to associate a closed mouth with the click.

EXTRA HELP

If a puppy keeps barking when you try to interrupt it the first time, you may have given the puppy too strong a stimulus to elicit his barking.

Step 4. Add the word signals "bark" and "quiet." (Turn to page 191 to review how to add a word signal to a behavior.)

Step 5. Practice and proof.

First, practice without any distractions present. Then, after the puppy understands the meaning of "bark" and "quiet," plan schooling sessions where you and the puppy can practice "bark" and "quiet." For example, ask a friend to ring your doorbell, meet you in the park while carrying an open umbrella, or walk a dog in front of your house.

THE SEVENTH PERFORMANCE PAIR: COME AND PLACE

"Come" requires puppies to stop what they are doing, join you, and stay with you until you release them. "Come" prevents puppies from leaving your property, chasing a cat, or getting hit by a car.

Happy, bouncy, energetic puppies need an "off" switch. After an active yang time, they need a quiet yin experience. "Place" means an active puppy settles down. It requires a puppy to move to a particular spot and remain there until you tell him "free." While the puppy is in this special area, he can sit, down, or shift positions. "Place" is not the same as "stay." "Stay" requires puppies to remain motionless in one specific position.

"Place" prevents begging at the dinner table, jumping on guests, running after children, or drooling on visitors. It creates a safe place for a dog in a busy house. "Place" also reduces separation anxiety, nervousness, and hyperactivity. It gives puppies a special area to relax, get away, and spend quiet time.

How to Teach Come

Silent trainers incorporate "come" every time they use the greeting ritual when they return to their puppy after a separation. (Turn to Chapter 15 to review the greeting ritual.) If you want to include additional "come" sessions using a clicker, try this.

Step 1. Play with the puppy. Walk a few feet away. When the puppy arrives at your feet, C/T.

Step 2. Say "free" to release the puppy.

Step 3. Repeat steps 1 and 2 until the puppy consistently runs to you.

Step 4. Add the word signal "come." (Turn to page 191 to review how to add a word signal to a behavior.)

Step 5. Continue to increase your distance from the puppy in small increments until you can stand twenty feet away, say "come," and the puppy runs to you. When the puppy arrives at your feet, C/T.

Step 6. To teach the puppy to stay near you after you call her, wait two seconds, then C/T. As you repeat this step, continue to increase the time the puppy must wait near you until you C/T. (This teaches a puppy that "come" means "stay with me until I release you.")

Step 7. Practice and proof. Move from inside the house to your backyard. Visit a friend who has a fenced backyard. Increase your distance. Add new distractions.

EXTRA HELP

If a puppy ignores you and starts to explore the room, find a way to stimulate the puppy's interest in you. Using a happy voice, say "puppy, puppy, puppy." Whistle, move, clap your hands, sit on the floor, or rhythmically tap your fingers on the tile. To shape "come," try this.

Step 1. The puppy lifts her ears; C/T.

Step 2. Looks at you or turns her head; C/T.

Step 3. Takes one step in your direction; C/T. As you repeat this step, continue to increase the number of steps a puppy must take before you C/T.

Step 4. Joins you; C/T.

Step 5. After the puppy consistently comes to you, add the word signal "come." (Turn to page 191 to review how to add a word signal to a behavior.)

Step 6. After the puppy comes to you, wait two seconds, then C/T. As you repeat this step, continue to increase the time the puppy waits until she hears C/T. (This teaches a puppy that "come" means "stay with me until I release you.")

How to Teach Place

Step 1. Place a rug, dog bed, or towel on the floor approximately one foot in front of you and the puppy.

Step 2. The puppy looks at the rug; C/T.

Step 3. Steps toward the rug; C/T.

Step 4. Reaches the rug; C/T.

Step 5. Puts front paws on the rug; C/T.

Step 6. Places all four paws on the rug; C/T.

Step 7. Say "free" to give the puppy permission to leave the rug.

Step 8. After the puppy regularly reaches and stands on the rug, wait to see what behavior the puppy offers next before you C/T. If the puppy offers a down, C/T. If not, say "down" after he stands on the rug. Then, C/T when he lies down.

Step 9. Add the word signal "place." (Turn to page 191 to review how to add a word signal to a behavior.) Gradually increase the length of time you expect the puppy to stay on the rug before you C/T.

Step 10. Move two feet from the rug, and say "place." After the puppy lies down on the rug, C/T.

Step 11. Practice and proof. Continue to increase the puppy's distance from the rug, until the puppy can find the rug and lie down on it from any location inside the house. Add distractions. Practice "place" during dinner, while you watch television, make lunch, fold clothes, or while the children play. Play with your puppy, and then tell him "place."

Note: Another way to teach a dog "place" is to set a target on top of the "place" rug. The puppy knows a target means "find, stand, and stare at the target to earn a reward." (Page 190 describes how to teach a puppy to find a target.)

Step 1. Say "get it." While the puppy stands on the rug, C/T.

Step 2. Say "free" to give the puppy permission to leave the rug.

Step 3. Add the word signal "place-get-it." (Turn to page 191 to review how to add a word signal to a behavior.)

Step 4. Remove the target.

Step 5. Say "place." While the puppy stands on the rug, C/T.

Step 6. Say "free."

Step 7. During the next learning sequence, wait before you C/T. See what behavior the puppy offers next. If the puppy offers a down, C/T. If not, say "down" after he stands on the rug. Then, C/T when he lies down.

Step 8. Say "place." Gradually increase the length of time you expect the puppy to stay on the rug before you C/T.

Step 9. Say "free."

Step 10. Move two feet from the rug, say "place." After the puppy lies down on the rug, C/T. Continue to increase the puppy's distance from the rug, until the puppy can find the rug and lie down on it from anywhere inside the house.

Step 11. Practice and proof. Increase the number of distractions. Practice "place" during dinner, while you watch television, make lunch, fold clothes, or the children play. Play with your puppy, and then tell him "place."

EXTRA HELP

Remember to say "free" to release the puppy from the rug between the different repetitions.

THE EIGHTH PERFORMANCE PAIR: WALK AND STAY

"Walk" asks puppies to walk quietly on-leash at your left side without pulling. "Walk" helps you move through crowd and visit the veterinarian, pet store, or park. As pack leader, a puppy follows you.

Note: Many people say "heel" instead of "walk." For me, heeling is a behavior required in obedience show rings. "Heel" means a dog walks with his head/shoulder area in perfect alignment with my left leg at all times. Instead, when I ask a puppy to "walk," it means that the dog stays close, does not pull on the leash, but is not tightly attached to my left side.

"Stay" requires puppies to remain motionless in one spot until you release them. "Stay" prevents puppies from jumping on visitors, running through open doors, or wandering if you stop and talk to someone. "Stay" comes in handy when you take a puppy with you and shop, travel, eat at an outdoor café, or visit with friends.

How to Teach Walk

Step 1. Start inside the house or garage. Hold the clicker in your right hand. Use your left hand to give the puppy a food reward. Move with active, forward, "happy" steps. Remember, puppies follow movement. As soon as the puppy reaches your side, C/T.

Step 2. Continue to walk and C/T when the puppy is near your left side. Make a big circle around the room. Reward frequently.

Step 3. Take a short play break.

Step 4. Make a big circle around the room in the opposite direction. C/T frequently.

Step 5. Take a short play break.

Step 6. Walk in a straight line and turn left; C/T during and immediately after the turn.

Step 7. Walk in a straight line and turn right; C/T during and immediately after the turn.

Step 8. Take a short play break.

Step 9. After a puppy consistently walks by your side, add the word signal "walk." (Turn to page 191 to review how to add a word signal to a behavior.)

Step 10. Add a leash. If the leash is short, loop it through your belt. If the leash is long, wrap and tie it around your waist, so that your feet and the puppy's feet cannot get tangled in it. Repeat steps 1 through 8. If the puppy runs forward and pulls against the leash, stop. Wait. When the puppy releases the pressure, C/T. After the C/T, change direction. Walk back briskly the way you came.

Step 11. Click/treat when the puppy reaches your left side again.

Step 12. Practice and proof. Practice on-leash. "Walk" in front of your house, during a trip around the block, at a friend's house, or at the park. Practice off-leash "walk" in an enclosed backyard, front yard, garage, basement, or friend's enclosed yard.

EXTRA HELP

If a puppy pulls strongly against the leash, include "loose leash" schooling sessions to teach him the value of a loose leash. Try this. Place a food treat on the ground about fifteen feet away as a distraction. Make sure the puppy knows the food is in front of him.

Step 1. With a short leash, walk toward the food. (A short leash prevents a puppy from running in front of you and eating the food treat.) If the puppy runs forward and pulls against the leash, stop. As soon as the puppy releases the pressure against the leash, C/T.

Step 2. After the C/T, change direction. Return the way you came. Walk briskly. Return to where you started the exercise.

Step 3. Walk toward the food. C/T for a loose leash. If the puppy runs forward and pulls against the leash, stop and repeat step 1.

Step 4. After releasing the pressure on the leash, increase the number of seconds that a puppy waits before you C/T.

Step 5. When the puppy walks the entire distance without pulling against the leash, say "take it" when the puppy reaches the food treat.

Step 6. Practice and proof. Change to a more appealing food or favorite food treat. This creates a bigger distraction for the puppy and tests whether the puppy has learned to walk without pulling. If a puppy is not interested in food, use a ball or toys as a distraction.

How to Teach Stay

Stay is a signal that can be used with a sit, stand, or down. The following steps assume the puppy knows how to sit or lie down at your signal.

An effortless way to teach "stay" is to increase the amount of time between when you ask for the "sit" or "down," and when you C/T. The puppy learns not to change positions until you release her. However, if you want to use the word signal "stay," try this.

Step 1. Ask a puppy to "sit," "down," or "stand" while you stand next to her. Say "stay." Then, say "free" to release the puppy from the stay. Build duration by varying the timing of your rewards. (See page 193 to review how to increase duration in a behavior.) During subsequent schooling sessions, increase the amount of time you ask the puppy to "stay" until the puppy stays by your side for one minute.

Step 2. After a puppy successfully stays by your side, increase the number and interest level of distractions in the schooling area. Build up to high-level distractions slowly. (See pages 194–95 to review how to add distractions.)

Step 3. Increase your distance. Move so you remain even with the dog, but now six inches separate you. Wait and C/T. Say "free."

Step 4. Continue to slowly increase your lateral distance until the puppy stays for one minute while you stand fifteen feet away.

Step 5. Practice and proof. Increase the number and interest level of distractions in the schooling area. Build up to high-level distractions slowly.

Step 6. Increase the distance between you and the puppy while you face the dog. Move six inches in front of the puppy, and say "stay." Wait and C/T. Say "free."

Step 7. Gradually increase your distance from the puppy until you can stand twenty-five feet away, and the puppy holds her position until you release her.

Step 8. Practice and proof.

In the beginning, practice "stay" in a quiet, secluded area. Then, add stationary distractions such as stuffed toys or your daughter quietly reading her book on the couch. Next, add moving distractions such as your son rolling a ball on the floor or playing with his toys. Build up the difficulty of the distractions slowly. Reward the puppy for maintaining her "stay" in the presence of distractions. Then, practice "stay" at different locations such as your backyard, front yard, or a friend's yard.

Extra Help

When you teach "stay," increase physical distance or increase the amount of time you expect the puppy to "stay," but do not increase distance and duration at the same time. Start by increasing the amount of time you ask for a stay, before you add distance. Use a puppy's favorite treat during the "stay" exercise. Remember to release the puppy from the stay by saying "free."

THE NINTH PERFORMANCE PAIR: INSIDE AND OUTSIDE

Puppies who understand "outside" and "inside" make house-training easy. "Outside" requires puppies to walk outside to eliminate. "Inside" means puppies eliminate in a litter box inside the house.

Defecating and urinating are natural behaviors. Your task is to teach a puppy where you want him to tinkle or poop. Creating a schedule and sticking to it speeds house-training. If you decide to feed the puppy breakfast at 6:00 A.M. during the weekdays, you should also feed him at 6:00 A.M. during the weekends.

Be proactive. Puppies need to eliminate every fifteen to thirty minutes during the day when they are awake. Take a puppy out after you wake up in the morning, before you go to bed at night, and when you come home from work. Watch for any circling, sniffing, scratching, whining, sudden restlessness, positioning by the door, or returning to the site of a previous accident that indicate a puppy needs to eliminate now. After puppies eat, wake up from a nap, or stop playing is a perfect time for an "inside" or "outside" schooling house-training session.

How to Teach Inside

You will need the following materials: litter box or plastic storage box, litter (absorbent pads, wood fiber pellets, commercial dog litter, paper, or newspaper), litter scoop, crate, exercise pen, clicker, and treats. Don't forget that a puppy must be able to easily step over the edge of a litter box. If you create an opening by sawing or cutting a plastic box, smooth the edge before you ask a puppy to use it.

Step 1. Cover the bottom of a litter box with one to two inches of litter, or place a pad or newspaper in the box. Over the top of a clean surface, place a previously used pad, newspaper, or feces. (After a puppy understands "inside—go potty" you will not have to "seed" the inside of the litter box.)

Extra Help

If you want to change from newspapers or absorbent pads to fiber wood pellets or other litter, do it gradually. Begin by placing a thin layer of litter near the front of the box, so that the surface is still mostly paper. Add more litter until eventually the entire newspaper is covered with a light layer of pellets or litter. Gradually increase the amount of litter until the newspaper is completely covered. Then, remove the paper.

Step 2. Depending on the size of the puppy, place the litter box inside an x-pen, laundry room, or large crate.

Step 3. After a puppy wakes up from a nap, playing, or eating, set the puppy inside the box. If the puppy urinates or defecates, C/T at its completion. (If the puppy does not eliminate, return the puppy to his crate. Do not allow a puppy to wander unsupervised. Watch the puppy for any signs that indicate she needs to eliminate.)

Step 4. Repeat step 3 until the puppy consistently eliminates inside the litter box.

Step 5. Add the word signal "spot"; C/T. (Turn to page 191 to review how to add a word signal to a behavior.)

Step 6. Teach the puppy to find the litter box. You may need to shape the behavior, i.e., look at the box, walk to the box, and step inside.

Step 7. Add another word signal, "inside"; C/T.

Step 8. Link the two word signals together. After a play session, say "inside—spot."

Step 9. When the puppy urinates or defecates, C/T at its completion.

EXTRA HELP

Keep a clicker and treats near the litter box. When you see the puppy use it on her own, say "inside–spot" in a soft voice while she urinates or defecates. Pair the C/T to coincide with the final drips!

In the first few weeks, always leave one pile and puddle inside the litter box to entice a puppy to return to the same place to eliminate. After a puppy demonstrates she knows "inside–spot," remove any waste at least twice a day. Use an enzymatic cleaner and completely clean and disinfect the litter box at least once a month.

How to Teach Outside

You will need the following items: dog collar, leash, clicker, and treats.

Step 1. After a puppy wakes up from a nap, playing, or eating, take the puppy outside. If the puppy urinates or defecates, C/T *at its completion.* If the puppy does not eliminate, return the puppy to his crate, or watch the puppy for any signs that indicate he needs to eliminate.

Step 2. Repeat step 1 until the puppy consistently eliminates outside.

Step 3. Add a word signal "spot," C/T. (Turn to page 191 to review how to add a word signal to a behavior.)

Step 4. Teach a puppy to signal you that he needs to go outside. Chapter 14 explains how to teach a puppy to ring a bell and add the word signal "outside."

Step 5. Link the two word signals "outside" and "spot" together. After a play session say, "outside—spot." Take the puppy outside.

EXTRA HELP

Do not punish accidents that happen inside the house. Instead, decrease the amount of time between outside bathroom visits. Find someone to help you house-train the puppy: a friend, neighbor, pet sitter, dog walker, or family member, or teach the puppy how to use a litter box or doggy door.

To teach a puppy how to use a doggy door, try this. If the doggy door has a vinyl flap, raise it so that it does not cover the opening. Have a friend hold the puppy in front of the doggy door. Walk outside and stand on the other side of the doggy door. Call the puppy's name. Most puppies will immediately walk through the opening; C/T. If the puppy does not move through the doggy door, shape the behavior. Click/treat the puppy's first step, second step, etc.

The next step requires that you partially obscure the doggy door opening with the flap. Call the puppy's name. Click/treat the puppy's arrival on the other side of the doggy door. If the puppy refuses to walk through, you are covering too much of the opening with the flap.

> The final step calls for the vinyl strips or sheet to completely cover the doggy door. Call the puppy's name. Click/treat the puppy's arrival on the other side of the doggy door. Then say, "go spot." When the dog eliminates, C/T.

When you follow the five practices that build good puppy behavior (see Chapter 19), you can solve problems, teach new behaviors, and raise a good dog easily. The key is to balance yin with yang. When you school "stay," a yin activity, pair it with "walk," a yang activity. Puppies learn more easily when behaviors are paired together.

Yin and yang are in constant motion. When yin expands, yang shrinks. When yang increases, yin decreases. Yin and yang constantly alter and change their relationship with each other; it happens all the time. During "come," a puppy who runs to you displays yang, but when she sits in front of you, that's yin. When the puppy moves behind you to reach your left side, she demonstrates yang. When she sits by your left side, it's yin. Although "come" is a yang activity, it contains yin aspects, i.e., the puppy sits in front of you and at your side. Yang acts. Yin waits.

Effective schooling sessions work with the dynamic of yin and yang to raise a good dog. If you have a wild, rambunctious yang puppy, teach her "place," a yin activity that settles a dog's energy. If a puppy runs away from you, teach "come." If a puppy jumps, teach "sit." Reward a yin "down-stay" with a yang ball toss.

Understanding the nature of yin and yang helps you teach any behavior; design effective learning sequences; create successful teaching strategies; find suitable rewards; discover appropriate distractions for your puppy; and adapt, alter, and work with your puppy's needs, desires, instincts, and drives. By balancing yin with yang, you raise a willing, confident, well-mannered puppy that practices self-control.

Part 5 | The Way of Play

Chapter 21
Games Puppies Play

W hat makes learning fun? Schooling sessions that feel like playtime. When puppies and people play games, everyone wins. You enjoy working with the puppy because it's challenging and fun. Puppies learn new ideas and skills quickly because it's exciting, not boring and repetitive.

Educational "play sessions" capture a puppy's attention, stimulate her mind, and strengthen bones and muscles. They use a canine's natural gifts of curiosity, risk taking, testing by trial and error, adaptability, and joy to stimulate learning and create a loving, merry bond between you and the puppy. Who says learning has to be dry, boring, and tedious? "Playing to learn" and "learning to play" follow a tao path that understands puppies are active social learners.

Puppies remind us that a tree branch, toy, ball, trip to the park, or visitor offer infinite opportunities for adventure, challenge, excitement, and fun. What is that smell? Who hid my toy? Where is the squirrel? How fast can I run? In the process of sniffing, chasing, eating, digging, or running, puppies learn. Play develops a puppy's social, mental, and physical abilities in a stress-free environment. It builds a puppy's confidence, trust, behavior, skills, and awareness. Play uses a puppy's natural curiosity, intelligence, and problem-solving abilities to teach new behaviors and good manners, and strengthen the relationship between you and your puppy.

When puppies play, they get up front, close, and personal. A quick nip there, a fast lunge here, a burst of energy, and puppies zoom around the yard, over each other, and run through a tunnel. The funny thing is, puppies do not care who runs fastest. They just want to have fun. I've watched the speediest puppy purposely slow down to keep another puppy in the chase.

Teaching is the art of organizing play. Puppies can learn anything with your guidance, time, and the right experiences. Schooling sessions that feel like playtime speed up the learning process because it's fun for puppies to observe, test, think, move, and interact. "Playing to learn" is the key to shaping a puppy's behavior effortlessly.

Play sessions help you, too. Playing refreshes and renews you. Worries disappear, exhaustion decreases, and happiness increases. You relax, trust the process, let go, and have fun. Your intuition guides you, and you and the puppy learn. You learn to think like a dog, meet a puppy on his terms, and recognize the importance of play in your life. The puppy learns new ways to act, think, move, and have fun.

Puppies learn while they play. "Playing to learn" actively involves puppies in the learning process as they observe, examine, test, search, and make choices. "Learning to play" teaches puppies new ways to cooperate, cope with challenging situations, and experience success. They discover new social skills and practice self-control. Puppies learn that words are signals; clicks, food, toys, balls, and games are great; specific behaviors bring rewards; and you are the leader. Educational play sessions help you channel raw puppy energy, stimulate a canine brain, and develop polished behaviors.

THE WAY OF PLAY

During play sessions you take a puppy's natural behaviors and work with them to create polished performances. Eight simple practices create successful playtime schooling sessions.

Note: Directions for playing specific games follow these guidelines.

1. Play reinforces leadership.

Leader starts and stops all games. She keeps in her possession any toys or balls at the end of a game. At the end of a session, they are not dropped on the floor for a puppy to play with and keep.

2. Play calls for common sense.

Do not play during potty time. Wait at least one hour after a puppy eats before playing. Avoid wrestling, roughhousing, combative, or violent play. Do not play games, such as chase the puppy, that cause the puppy to think he is leader.

Use your body, hands, and legs as guides, not as play toys. Never allow puppies to tug on your hands, arms, body, or clothes. Teach puppies to "leave it" and "tug." (Turn to pages 205–208 to learn how to teach "leave it." Turn to page 213 to learn how to teach tug.)

3. Play begins with one dog at a time.

In the beginning, separate other dogs or animals from your play area. Introduce games to each dog separately. After each dog knows the game, add other family members and dogs.

Games: "Tail Wagging," "Red Light/Green Light," "Tic Tac Toe," "Musical Paws," "Follow the Leader," "Craters in the Moon," "Alphabet Walking," and "Popcorn Popper" lend themselves to group participation.

4. Play stimulates puppies.

Throwing a ball for five minutes neither exhausts nor relaxes puppies. Running, fetching, and chasing activities rev up puppies. Yin puppies need the stimulation and excitement that games provide. However, yang puppies need to learn how to balance play with quiet times. Remember to play in short sessions with high-energy dogs.

The best play sessions include yin behaviors with yang events, and yang behaviors with yin events. For example, include work on "place" between games with a yang puppy. (Turn to page 218 to learn how to teach "place.")

Games: "Red Light/Green Light," "Popcorn Popper," "Tic Tac Toe," and "Musical Paws" teach puppies how to balance activity with quiet.

5. Play motivates puppies.

Your attitude when you play rouses a puppy's interest. Act enthusiastic. Laugh. Clap your hands, whistle, cheer, and have a good time. Take light, bouncy steps: skip, run, jump up and down, or hop. During a game, if a puppy becomes over-excited, cowers, or hides, decrease your intensity. Use a softer voice, move less, and make less dramatic gestures. Plan shorter sessions.

Games: "Tail Wagging," "Hide and Seek," "Musical Paws," and "Doggy Dancing" stimulate a puppy's attitude.

Note: To calm and focus yang puppies, include a session of "Alphabet Walking" between games.

6. Play builds confidence.

Timid yin puppies that hide behind chairs, cringe, or constantly send "calming signals" need games that draw them out.

Games: "Find Me," "Hide and Seek," and "Tail Wagging" build a puppy's courage, trust, and self-assurance.

7. Play decreases chewing, destructive behavior, and anxiety.

Playing channels a puppy's energy in constructive ways. However, after playing, do not immediately confine puppies to a crate or laundry room. Wait. Take a few moments and spend a little quiet time with the puppy. Gently pet her. Stroke your hand down the puppy's back. Rub around her ears. Give her some time and space to settle down. Then, if you cannot supervise the puppy, place her in a crate, exercise pen, or room.

Games: "Red Light/Green Light," "Follow the Leader," "Craters in the Moon," "Alphabet Walking," and "Hide and Seek" redirect and focus a puppy's energy.

8. Play builds muscles and bones.

A puppy's body needs protecting. Do not ask puppies to leap for Frisbees, jump for balls, spring over jumps, or go on a two-mile run.

Games: "Find Me," "Craters in the Moon," and "Doggy Dancing" strengthen canine structure without physical stress.

ELEVEN GAMES TO PLAY WITH A PUPPY

The following games have been tested, examined, and analyzed by playful boxers, cattle dogs, terriers, spaniels, miniature pinschers, golden retrievers, Labrador retrievers, German shepherds, and other enthusiastic, eager "gamers." Decide which games fit with you, your puppy, and your lifestyle. Then, choose a game and play it with your puppy. If necessary, modify, adapt, or change a game based on what your puppy requires. Or, create new games or special events designed for your puppy's particular interests and needs. Help puppies "learn to play" and "play to learn" by incorporating the following games into your schooling sessions: "Tail Wagging," "Hide and Seek," "Find Me," "Red Light/Green Light," "Tic Tac Toe," "Musical Paws," "Doggy Dancing," "Alphabet Walking," "Craters in the Moon," "Follow the Leader," and "Popcorn Popper."

1. "Tail Wagging." Act happy. Squeak a toy. Wiggle food in front of the puppy's face. When the puppy wags her tail, C/T. If your puppy does not have a tail, moving her rear end back and forth counts as a tail wag. If you have more than one dog, teach each dog how to wag her tail. Then, have a contest. Who wags her tail the fastest? Longest? With the most motion?

"Tail Wagging" motivates, builds confidence, focus, and attention.

2. "Hide and Seek." Hide a toy or ball. Make it easy. At first, hide the ball in plain sight. For example, put it two feet in front of the puppy, next to a chair leg, or under an ottoman. Then, say "get the ball!" As the game progresses, hide the ball in more challenging locations, such as under a dresser, behind a door, or under the edge of an area rug. This is a great game for children to play with you. Ask them to hide the ball for the puppy.

"Hide and Seek" teaches "fetch," "stay," "gentle," and "take it." It motivates, builds confidence, and channels a puppy's energy positively. (To learn how to teach "fetch," "stay," "gentle," and "take it," review Chapter 20.)

3. "Find Me." If a puppy does not know how to stay, ask a friend to hold the puppy while you hide until you call the dog's name. Happily shout the puppy's name: "China!" Clap your hands or whistle to lead her to you. In the beginning, hide in obvious places. When the puppy finds you, praise and reward. After the puppy understands the game and easily discovers your hiding places, add the word "come." Say "China, come!"

As the game progresses, find more challenging locations to hide, such as behind a bathroom door, under a table, or next to a desk. When you play "hide and seek" outside, conceal yourself behind a tree, row of bushes, or in a toolshed with the door left open. Children are experts at discovering potential hiding places.

(To learn how to teach "stay" and "come," review Chapter 20.)

"Find Me" develops self-assurance, strong muscle and bones, and practices stay and come.

4. "Red Light/Green Light." This game requires at least two people to play it. One person, Nancy, acts as the stoplight and calls out "red light" or "green light." The second person, Jeremy, has the puppy, Beamer, on-leash. The goal is for Jeremy and Beamer to reach Nancy without being returned to the start line. Nancy, the "stoplight," stands twenty or thirty feet away and turns 180 degrees so she cannot see Jeremy and the puppy. Nancy keeps her back turned and calls out "green light." Jeremy walks with the puppy while the light is green. When Nancy calls out "red light," Jeremy stops moving and asks the puppy to sit. If the puppy is not sitting by the time Nancy turns around, Jeremy and Beamer must return to the start line.

"Red Light/Green Light" balances yin (quiet) with yang (movement), within the same activity. It channels a puppy's energy in a constructive manner and teaches "sit," "down," and "settle."

EXTRA HELP

With puppies that are just learning to sit, it helps if the person designated as stoplight counts, "One, two, three," before saying "red light." It provides additional time for the puppy handler to stop and ask the puppy to sit before the person says "red light" and turns around. (To learn how to teach "sit," "down," or "walk," review Chapter 20.)

Start with the handler walking. Then change to skipping, hopping, and running steps.

In the beginning, ask puppies to sit. During the next traffic session, ask puppies to lie down. In future sessions, ask for tricks such as play bow, shake, or crawl.

---

5. **"Tic Tac Toe."** Draw the lines for a huge tic tac toe game on the ground with chalk, use a light nylon cord to form lines, or drag a stick in the ground to make furrows. Make the squares large, approximately four feet by four feet. The squares must be big enough so that a person can stand next to a dog while he lies down or sits in the square, without crowding the people and dogs in other squares.

"Tic Tac Toe" can be played with one puppy, three dogs, or nine dogs. It can be played with two people, one adult and four children, or any combination of up to nine adults and children. Remember, someone can stand in a square without a puppy. If you have fewer than nine people, use a paper plate to indicate "O," and a sheet from a roll of paper towels to designate "X."

Two people control the placement of the Xs and Os. The "X" person asks a puppy and handler to go to a square and "sit-stay." Then, the "O" person asks a dog and handler to go to a square and "sit-stay." The game is played until there are three Xs or Os in a line, or it's a draw. After you complete a game, change who calls "X" or "O" first, and play again. Then, ask the dogs to "down-stay."

The advanced version of this game places dogs in a "stay" and leaves them in a square without a person standing next to them. (To learn how to teach "sit," "down," "stay," or "walk," review Chapter 20.)

"Tic Tac Toe" teaches puppies how to balance activity and quiet, reinforces leadership, and teaches puppies they can "sit-stay" and "down-stay" in the presence of other dogs and people.

6. "Musical Paws." This game requires at least two people to play it. One person starts and stops the music. The second person walks with the puppy on-leash.

Start with four chairs, set eight feet apart. Turn on the music. During the music, the person and puppy "walk the square." When the music stops, the person must run to the closest chair and ask the puppy to sit or lie down for fifteen seconds. Then, the music starts and it's time to walk the square again. This game is more fun with two, three, or four puppies. Always include enough chairs for all the players. (To learn how to teach "sit," "down," "settle," or "walk," review Chapter 20.)

The advanced version of this game spaces the chairs fifteen to thirty feet apart until there is a chair in each corner of a fenced backyard.

"Musical Paws" balances yang activity with yin relaxation. It teaches puppies how to have an "off" switch. It increases enthusiasm, motivates, and teaches "sit," "down," "walk," and "settle." It also establishes your role as pack leader.

7. "Doggy Dancing." Turn on happy music and start "dancing." With the puppy next to your side, run, walk, hop, or skip. Circle right, circle left, or back up. Insert a "sit" or "down" between the changes in tempo. Teach a puppy to spin to the left and twist to the right. Improvise, invent, and dance!

"Doggy Dancing" spurs a puppy's attention and focus; builds muscles and bones; practices "sit," "down," and "walk"; and makes learning fun! (To learn how to teach "sit," "down," or "walk," review Chapter 20.)

8. "**Alphabet Walking.**" Draw a large (at least eight-foot-high) letter of the alphabet on the ground with spray chalk, masking tape, or by digging a furrow in the dirt with a stick. You are going to walk with the puppy on-leash over the letter. Any place where the lines intersect, the puppy must "sit" or "down." At the beginning and end of a letter, the puppy must "sit" or "down." Start easy. Walk an "S." Then, try an "L," "D," or "N." (To learn how to teach "sit," "down," "settle," or "walk," review Chapter 20.)

"Alphabet Walking" calms and focuses a puppy's attention. It practices "sit," "down," "walk," and "settle."

9. "**Craters in the Moon.**" Design an obstacle course for a puppy to go over and through. Possible obstacles include: a ladder lying on the ground, an open umbrella, a blue plastic tarp, a "bridge" made out of a two-by-ten-by-twelve-foot board placed on two cement blocks (one block should be placed under each end), a children's play tunnel, or a "table" made out of a four-by-four-foot plywood board resting on four cement blocks (one block should be under each corner). Use your imagination to create obstacles. You can crush and twist paper grocery bags and lay them on the ground, make a pile of cardboard boxes, or modify children's play equipment. (To learn how to teach "walk," review Chapter 20.)

"Craters in the Moon" improves attention and focus. Puppies learn how to deal with distractions and challenges. They find new ways to move, think, and interact. Playing "Craters in the Moon" channels a puppy's energy, builds his awareness, and works with "up," "off," and "walk." (To learn how to teach "up," "off," and "walk," review Chapter 20.)

10. "**Follow the Leader.**" Line up single file. One person leads for thirty seconds. For example, you walk with the puppy on-leash around chairs, up and down stairs, or around tables. Then, you sit on a chair and ask the puppy to "sit." Next, you might lie on the floor and ask the puppy to "down." After you have finished playing "Follow the Leader," another person can take the lead for thirty seconds with the puppy.

When you play follow the leader outside, walk around bushes, trees, or playhouses. Lie down on the grass and ask the puppy to "sit." Sit and ask the puppy to "down." (To learn how to teach "sit," "down," or "walk," review Chapter 20.)

"Follow the Leader" reinforces your position as leader. It increases attention and focus and builds a puppy's confidence. It works with a puppy's ability to listen and handle a variety of situations.

11. "**Popcorn Popper.**" Play this game *after* the puppy successfully performs "sit," "stay," "down," "leave it," "gentle," and "free" and has demonstrated self-control in other games. Gather your children together. Explain that the puppy must learn how to act around them. This game teaches a puppy how to deal with running, playing, and jumping children. Explain that the game starts with one child at a time. Increase the number of children and the intensity of their activity slowly! Only do this activity with one puppy at a time.

Describe how heat causes popcorn to "pop." Tell children the room you are in is the "popcorn popper." When you say "pop," one child can run around the room. When you say "snack time," the child must stop in his tracks. If the puppy is running with him, the child tells the puppy to "sit." When the puppy sits, the child gives the puppy a treat. Then, the child says "free" to release the puppy from his sit. Repeat. When the puppy can handle one child playing, add two or three children. The child who stands closest to the puppy says "sit" and gives the puppy a treat.

Start with short, five-to-ten-second "pop" sessions. Increase the time the "popcorn pops" until children can run and play for sixty seconds and the puppy immediately sits when the child says "sit." (To learn how to teach "sit," "down," "settle," or "walk," review Chapter 20.)

EXTRA HELP

When children and puppy successfully play the game, increase the amount of time between when a puppy sits and the delivery of the treat.

"Popcorn Popper" teaches puppies how to balance yang activity with yin quiet. It also schools "sit," "walk," and "free." It helps puppies learn how to relax and settle around children.

Play tests and teaches. It stimulates puppies to learn, explore, and follow the leader. Play is not work. Instead, the way of play is easy, effective, natural, and fun. It helps puppies develop mentally, physically, and emotionally. Play creates a strong bond between you and your puppy. During play sessions, puppies learn how to interact with people, objects, other animals, distractions, and challenging situations. The more you play, the more the puppy learns. When you follow the "Way of Play," it makes you and your puppy happy, resilient, and wise.

Chapter 22
Yappy Hour

Monday evening, Helen called and said, "Let's get together." I imme-diately knew what she meant. No, it wasn't a trip to the spa, movies, lunch, or shopping. It was time to arrange a "play date" with her two Aus-tralian shepherds, Lacey and Hap, and my border collie, Jet. Lacey, Hap, and Jet met in my puppy kindergarten class. Eleven months later we still arrange play dates for our dogs.

Yappy hours introduce puppies to new dogs, children, and adults. People yappy hours introduce puppies to other adults and children. Puppy yappy hours introduce puppies to other dogs. Do not wait until a puppy has completed all of his shots to socialize him. Instead, socialize your puppy with your friends' and neighbors' dogs that are healthy and current on their vaccinations.

Yappy hours can take any form. Tiffany hung black-and-white bal-loons inside her house to celebrate the arrival of her newest Dalmatian. You can send out invitations in the shape of a dog bone, e-mail your friends, or call them on the phone. Invite friends, family, neighbors, and healthy puppies to meet the newest member of your family and help you socialize her. Then, ask your friends, neighbors, and relatives if you can visit them with your puppy. From the beginning, puppies need to be ex-posed to other people's animals and new environments. If you do not take puppies out of their house or yard, their narrow definition of home and fa-miliarity can create antisocial, timid, wary, or unfriendly dogs.

PEOPLE YAPPY HOURS

People yappy hours introduce puppies to other people and children. Puppies meet people who touch, hold, brush, love, and play with them. Hold a yappy hour for your puppy. Invite friends and family to meet the newest member of your family. To create a safe party environment, ask guests to take off their shoes before entering the house to prevent the puppy from being exposed to any contagious diseases. Give each person some of the puppy's favorite treats in a plastic baggie. Then, ask them to sit on the floor or in the grass outside in the backyard. Invite three or four people so you can make a small circle.

When everyone is seated, bring in the puppy on-leash. Take off her leash and sit with her on your lap while everyone chats. After the puppy comfortably settles in your lap, look at the person who is sitting near you and say, "Would you like to hold my puppy?" The person can clap his hands, whistle, or run his fingers through the carpeting or grass while he says the puppy's name. If the puppy does not willingly leave you, bring the puppy to the person. Then, let the new person talk to and touch the puppy. Then, the new person passes the puppy to the next person.

Depending on the puppy's personality, you might stop with one trip around the circle. Or, you might pass the puppy again. This time people might look in the puppy's ears and touch and gently hold each paw. During future yappy hours people can brush the puppy, ask the puppy to "sit" or "down," and wear gloves, funny hats, Halloween masks, or crinkly raincoats.

As the puppy grows in confidence, at future yappy hours play "Alphabet Walking," "Hide and Seek," "Find Me," or "Follow the Leader."

PUPPY YAPPY HOURS

To hold a puppy yappy hour at your house, invite two or three people to bring their puppies to your house for a puppy party. All the dogs should

Pass the puppies during puppy yappy hour.

be close to the same age. Invite puppies who are four, five, or six months old. Do not invite a ten-month-old dog to hang out with your three-month-old puppy.

The best place for yappy hour is outdoors on grass. Then, if a puppy eliminates, no one needs to run for an enzymatic cleaner to clean the carpet.

Touch the puppy's feet.

Look in the puppy's ears.

Open the puppy's mouth.

The area must be fenced and puppy-proofed. At our house, we have a twenty-five-by-twenty-five-foot fenced grass enclosure that works perfectly for puppy parties. Make sure there are some chairs or tables to give a shy puppy somewhere safe to watch the events. To create a safe party environment, ask guests to take off their shoes before entering the grassy area to prevent a puppy from being exposed to any contagious diseases.

Ask each person to sit on the grass with the puppy. Give each person some puppy treats in a plastic baggie. Start by passing each puppy to a new person. Look in their ears, open their mouths, and touch their feet. Then, pass them on to the next person. This gives the puppies the opportunity to meet new people, settle in, and be near new dogs without directly interacting with them.

Stand up. Release puppies one at a time to play. If one puppy appears very dominant and intimidating, "buddy up." (Chapter 15 explains how to buddy up.) You can also remove the puppy from the play group by placing him on-leash and allowing the more mellow puppies to play together. Then, release the yang puppy again.

"Walk," "sit," and "down" on "bridge."

During a puppy yappy hour, alternate two-to-three-minute play sessions with short schooling sessions, where puppies practice "sit," "down," "up," and "off," or "tunnel" and "bridge." Include games such as "Red Light/Green Light," "Tic Tac Toe," or "Musical Paws."

Puppy and people yappy hours create confident, social puppies who interact easily with adults, children, strangers, and other dogs.

Tunnel.

Chapter 23
Face-to-Face: Introducing Children and Puppies

Ethan, Taylor, Emily, and Madison sit at their mother's feet while Jenna reads to them from a book about puppies. At the end of the story, Jenna asks, "What did you learn about living with a puppy?"

"Puppies don't like to be picked up by their tails," Ethan replied.

"Puppies like to run," said Emily.

"Marigold needs friends," said Taylor.

"Madison, what do you think?" asked Jenna.

"Puppies lick you because they love you," Madison answered.

"Next week we pick up our new Labrador retriever puppy," Jenna said.

"Will she look like Marigold?" asked Emily.

"Yes. Her name is Buttercup. I have a stuffed dog here. Let's practice picking up the puppy and holding and touching her." Jenna and the children spend the next twenty minutes talking about Buttercup: how to hold, play, feed, brush, give her a treat, and pet her. For the next five days, Jenna plans a daily activity and mini-discussion about how to live with, love, and care for a puppy. Early Saturday morning the entire family drives to the breeder's house to pick up Buttercup.

Puppies and children are lively, spirited, active, and intense. Small children run, jump, talk with a high-pitched voice, and use quick, jerky movements. Active, bouncy, happy puppies leap, bite, nip, chase, and run. Both children and puppies are playful, reactive, and movement-oriented. They distract easily, have short attention spans, and need time to rest. Combine them without preparation, rules, or supervision, and chaos erupts.

Parents need to teach children how to safely interact with puppies because children's movements often unsettle, threaten, and provoke puppies.

Parents need to teach puppies how to safely interact with children because a puppy's actions may disturb and harass children. However, if you take the time to calmly and safely introduce puppies and children, you can prevent accidents, injuries, and hurt feelings.

Am I extra cautious about children and puppies living together? You bet. I'm the person who had to evaluate the small white dog after he bit the seven-year-old's face, and she needed fourteen stitches. The parents exercised poor judgment and allowed the little girl and dog to walk in the neighborhood without supervision. *Always supervise children and dogs.* There are no exceptions to this rule. Dogs are not furry babysitters. Do not allow children and puppies to sleep together at night.

You must teach puppies and children how to act around each other. With constant supervision, you can intervene quickly before a situation gets out of control. Three practices keep children and puppies safe and out of trouble.

1. *Always* stay within an arm's length of puppies and children.

2. Avoid overwhelming puppies with too many children, activities, or attendance at a special event. For example, puppies act differently when they visit your sister's family, play in a dog park, attend baseball semi-finals, or run in the backyard with six children practicing soccer.

3. Adults reprimand puppies, never children. You are pack leader. You are the only one who should "buddy up" with the puppy when he needs to make a different choice. A dog's natural inclination is to treat children as pack mates or prey. Children often act like prey animals. They run, scream, and talk in high-pitched voices that stimulate the canine hunting instinct.

A child can never be pack leader. Although some children are bossy, their actions lack authority. They are too short, shrill, and sharp. When faced with problems, many children get angry, hit, scream, or use force.

Very young children (up to four or five years old) and young children (five to nine years old) can help you teach a puppy. Children who are ten years and older can teach a puppy while you watch. Evaluate the maturity level of your child. One six-year-old child may have expert hands and a gentle soul. Another six-year-old child may act rough and have no patience. Pay attention to how your children interact with other children. It will help you determine their role in raising the puppy and the lessons you need to emphasize. Although children can help you with the puppy, it's not their job. It's your responsibility.

To teach children about puppies, tell them, and then show them what you mean. Use stuffed animals, stories, videos, and hands-on experiences to get across your message. Five habits will help your children and puppy live happily ever after. Teach children to:

1. Look for an adult.

2. Seek permission.

3. Touch softly.

4. Act carefully.

5. Play smart.

1. Look for an adult.

Teach children that when they are with the puppy, you or another adult must be present.

Rule: It takes three to play.

2. Seek permission.

Instruct children to seek your permission before they do anything with or to a puppy.

Rule: Ask first, play later.

3. Touch softly.

Children don't know their own strength. Teach them how to gently touch puppies. Then, show children where puppies like to be touched. For example, encourage children to pet a puppy's shoulders or scratch under his chin. Practice petting the puppy every day until your children understand how to touch softly.

Rule: Soft as a feather, smooth as silk.

An easy way to demonstrate where puppies like to be touched is to show your child on his own body. Pat your son on his head at least six or eight times. Ask him, "Do you like how this feels?" When he answers "no," explain puppies do not like pats on their heads either. Next, rub softly down his back. Ask him again, "Do you like how this feels?" When he says "yes," explain that puppies like to be rubbed down their back from the shoulders to their tail.

To teach your daughter the value of a gentle caress, ask her to put her arm (from her elbow to her hand) flat against the kitchen table. Explain that first you will demonstrate a perfect puppy touch—light, gentle, friendly, and soothing. Next, you will pat harder on her arm. Ask which touch she likes better. Discuss that puppies prefer soft, friendly touches rather than pats, slaps, or strikes. Then, hold the puppy and ask your daughter to touch him. Place a young child's hand inside your hand and help her pet the puppy.

4. Act carefully.

Teach children to respect a puppy's body, territory, food, and toys. Explain that a puppy can guard his toys, bones, or food bowl. Discuss that a puppy might bite if children surprise him while he sleeps in his bed or crate. Teach children that if a puppy is sick, to leave him alone. Remind them that their actions can frighten puppies, and scared, worried, or startled puppies might growl, nip, or bite them if they:

A. Reach over the puppy's head to pet the puppy.

B. Poke fingers or anything else into a puppy's eyes, ears, or body.

C. Hit, kick, grab, pinch, squeeze, tease, or pull fur, ears, or tail.

D. Step on the puppy.

E. Toss a puppy into a swimming pool, off a deck, or into a snowbank.

F. Walk or sneak up behind a puppy.

G. Run at a puppy while he sleeps.

H. Threaten, disturb, or corner puppies.

Talk with your children about the best way to greet a puppy. Teach them to say the puppy's name, clap their hands, or whistle to let a puppy know they want to say "hi" or play. Tell them to wake up a sleeping puppy by first calling his name.

Show children how to handle, hold, and carry a puppy. Discuss why tight hands that grasp fur can cause puppies to nip, bite, or struggle to get away.

Rule: Easy does it.

Hunter picks up a puppy carefully.

Teach children how to hold a puppy. Explain that a puppy's front and back end both need support. Ask older children to sit on the floor while you place the puppy in their lap. Sit younger children in your lap so you can help them hold the puppy. Explain that they should only hold the puppy when they sit on the floor.

How to Pick Up a Puppy

1. Place one hand under the puppy's chest.

2. Tuck the other hand under the puppy's rear end.

3. Support the puppy's front and back end as you gently lift the puppy.

4. Rest the puppy against your chest. Use your arms to provide additional support.

5. Do not walk or run with a puppy in your arms.

Teach children how to give a treat to the dog. First, teach the puppy "take it," "leave it," and "gentle." Second, explain to your daughter not to stick out her hand with a treat, and as the puppy starts to grab it, to quickly withdraw her hand. Instead, explain she needs to stretch out her hand and wait for the puppy to take the treat. Third, place your daughter's hand inside your hand and practice "take it" and "leave it." Finally, let her give the puppy a treat without your assistance. Turn to pages 207–208 to learn how to teach "take it" and "leave it," and page 211 to teach "gentle."

EXTRA HELP

Remind children to never take food, toys, or balls from a puppy's mouth.

5. Play smart.

Kids just want to have fun. Puppies want to play. And some games are better than other games. Instead of children playing tug-of-war, chase me, or rough wrestling activities that stimulate a puppy's predator instincts, children can play fetch or hide-and-seek games that work with a dog's drives and focus his instincts in a positive direction. Chapter 21 lists games for puppies and children to play.

Rule: Fun is best when it's shared.

If a puppy gets too excited, stop the activity or game. Children playing, laughing, yelling, or rolling on the floor can overstimulate dogs and cause them to nip, yip, run, leap, and act wild.

Teach children if they get scared by a puppy's behavior to stand up straight, wrap their arms around their body, look up at the sky or ceiling, and "freeze." Instead of screaming or yelling, tell them to sing a song quietly until you can take care of the situation. If a child is knocked over by a dog, tell him to curl into a tight little ball, tuck his chin next to his chest, cover his head with his arms, and sink against the floor or ground until you tell him to get up.

EXTRA HELP

Remind children: no wrestling or teasing a puppy; do not stare into a dog's eyes; and never play with or pet a growling, snarling, or teeth-baring dog.

Seven days a week, twenty-four hours a day, puppies are ready to share their love, joy, and playfulness with you and your children. With your help, children and puppies can run, play, rest, and live happily together—each one helping the other to trust, learn, begin a new adventure, find treasure, exchange secrets, and face the world with a best friend.

Share puppies with your children.

Chapter 24
Face-to-Face: Introducing Puppies to Dogs, Cats, and Horses

Pip's introduction started slowly in our house. Pip, a border collie rescue dog, hid under our bed. She was afraid to walk into our kitchen or bathroom. She barked when she met my husband, Jeff.

The first time Pip met Zoe Samantha, the dogs were on the opposite side of a five-foot mesh fence. Jeff walked Zoe on-leash, and I walked Pip on-leash on our respective sides of the fence. As we walked along the fence, they saw each other, but did not interact with each other. When we stopped walking, we allowed them to meet and sniff noses through the fence. After a few days, Zoe and Pip were comfortable seeing each other through the fence. We opened the gate and walked them near each other. More days passed. We took Zoe off-leash while I walked Pip. Then, we took Pip off-leash, while Jeff walked Zoe. Finally, we took them both off-leash at the same time. They sniffed noses, ran, barked, chased, and played. Taking our time paid off. Today, Zoe and Pip are best friends.

Introductions are important at our house. A puppy must meet large adult dogs; Minerva, our orange tabby cat; and deal with the presence of five horses. Two guidelines smooth the entry of a new puppy into any family: 1. Plan ahead; and 2. Act with awareness of canine, feline, and equine natures.

Plan Ahead

You have done your homework, researched the breed, found a responsible breeder, paid attention to the parents, assessed the puppy's living conditions, and evaluated the puppy. A new puppy is joining your household and she matches your lifestyle, family, and interests. Two weeks before your resident cats and dogs meet the puppy face-to-face, introduce her smell by bringing towels, rugs, or toys from the breeder's house that are covered with the puppy's scent.

> *Note: When the puppy arrives at your house, take some time to get to know her. Plan on spending at least one hour with the puppy every day, apart from the other dogs and cats. You and the puppy need time to establish your relationship. Start teaching the puppy the nine performance pairs (see Chapter 20) during your time together. They will come in handy when the puppy meets new dogs, cats, horses, rabbits, squirrels, or birds.*

Introduce the puppy to each resident dog, one at a time. After the puppy meets everyone individually, introduce the puppy into the pack. Start with the two most laid-back members of your pack. Let the three of them "meet and greet." As time passes, continue to add additional pack members until the puppy runs with the entire pack. Plan on this process taking *at least* one to two weeks.

The best introductions occur in a neutral location. Every house has an area that your resident dogs do not normally visit: a garage, spare bedroom, or front yard. These areas are neutral grounds. Find a neutral location to introduce the puppy to your resident adult dog(s). If it is ninety-five degrees, raining, or snowing outside, meet inside. If weather permits, meet outside in a neutral location, such as a neighbor's or friend's fenced yard. If you introduce the puppy and dog at a park, go to a park that your adult dog does not normally visit.

Introducing two dogs to each other requires two people. One person has the puppy on-leash, the other person has the adult dog on-leash. Keep the leashes loose! A tight leash telegraphs that you are worried or concerned. Keep your voices light and happy.

First, the person with the puppy walks to the far side of the neutral area—for example, the front yard—and waits at the far end. Then, the second person walks into the front yard with the adult dog and stays at the near end. Give the dog and puppy enough distance from each other so they can look at each other but not be confronted by the other's presence. Reward quiet, calm, and relaxed behavior with a click/treat or food.

Gradually walk the two dogs closer together. The next step depends on the dogs. When Red and Trevor met each other for the first time, it was not meeting a stranger, but meeting a best friend. One sniff, a lick, two tails wagged in harmony, and they were friends for life.

Other dogs need more time to adjust to the presence of a new puppy. Gradual introductions are effective with hesitant, shy, or wary dogs. The process may take several days or weeks. Meet in a neutral location and start by walking both dogs in the same direction around the perimeter of the front yard. In the beginning, walk in a large circle. Keep plenty of space between the dog and puppy.

Change directions as you walk, so that at first the adult dog leads walking one way, then the puppy leads when you change directions. Reward quiet, calm, and relaxed behavior with a click/treat or food.

Gradually decrease the size of the circle, which will decrease the space between the dogs. Continue to reward good behavior. Eventually move so that you and the other person end up standing next to each other, side by side. Allow the two dogs to "sniff and greet" each other. After a short time, separate them. Walk the circle and meet again, allowing the dogs to interact. Take as many sessions as needed until both dogs are comfortable with each other.

When both dogs meet, greet, and remain calm in the other dog's presence, take the adult dog off-leash. If the adult dog remains quiet and relaxed and interacts with the puppy nicely, you are ready for the next step. If the adult dog does not remain calm, but reacts negatively, put the leash back on him. Increase your distance and repeat the previous steps. This process may take many sessions.

When the adult dog stays calm off-leash in the puppy's presence, you are ready to take the puppy off-leash. However, first reattach the adult dog's leash. Now, take the puppy off-leash. The puppy will probably greet and sniff the adult dog. If the adult dog remains quiet and relaxed, take both dogs off-leash. If he does not, reattach the puppy's leash, increase your distance, and repeat the previous steps. Remember, this process may take many sessions. If you have any concerns about either dog's behavior, seek professional assistance.

Supervise the adult dog and puppy closely. Let them meet, greet, and play. After a few minutes, separate them.

During this introduction exercise, reward positive behavior frequently. Take as many sessions as needed until both dogs are comfortable with each other.

After the puppy and adult dog are at ease meeting in a neutral zone, bring them to your backyard. Repeat the previous process. After the backyard sessions go smoothly, introduce the puppy and dog in the house. Plan "time-out" breaks. Use crates, baby-gates, or laundry rooms to allow the puppy and dog to have time and space away from each other.

Note: Never leave a puppy alone with an adult dog until you are 100 percent certain that the two dogs are completely compatible.

If you think a puppy or dog might react unpleasantly, introduce the dogs through a fence where they can see but not reach the other dog. Start with on-leash walking on separate sides of the fence. After the dogs are comfortable seeing each other through the fence, open the gate and begin the circular walking, meeting, and greeting process previously mentioned.

Note: If you are introducing a puppy to potentially reactive dogs or cats, seek professional help.

Give the puppy and current resident dog(s) plenty of time and space to prevent any possible friction. For example, separate dogs during mealtimes. If you have two dogs, use two food bowls. If you have three dogs, use three food bowls. Do not place four dog dishes next to each other on the floor. One dog will push another dog away from her food bowl so he can eat it, too. Move food bowls so each dog has a separate eating area. In our house, Logan and Red eat in the kitchen. Pip eats outside the kitchen under a counter. Zoe and Jet eat inside their crates.

Puppies usually need to eat more frequently than adult dogs. However, that does not mean that adult dogs don't want to eat another meal. Avoid problems by feeding a puppy in a crate or in the laundry room and closing the door while she eats her extra meal.

Adult dogs and puppies take time to accept each other. Do not hurry or force an introduction between canines. Remember, there is a time to act and a time to wait. A time for space and a time for togetherness. A time to advance and a time to retreat.

When you bring the puppy home, be prepared to accept the fact that the other dogs or cats may not share your excitement about the puppy. In the case of dogs, the reason is simple: the puppy does not look like a doggy playmate. When Red met Logan for the first time, he sniffed him and walked away. Two weeks later, they were best friends.

Logan and Zoe spend quiet time together.

Recognize that a puppy's temperament also influences the other dog's reactions. When Zoe Samantha first saw Red, she submissively peed and howled in terror. Red ran away. He wanted no part of this screaming creature. However, by the second introduction session, Zoe and Red changed their minds. Today, Zoe and Red play tug with each other. Each dog takes one end of a rope toy, and they pull each other across the tile floor.

ACT WITH AWARENESS OF CANINE, FELINE, AND EQUINE NATURES

All dogs are intrigued by other animals because they smell and look different. Frequently, cats, birds, squirrels, and horses run away when a puppy moves toward them. However, your attitude and position as pack leader can control whether a puppy chases the cat or ignores her.

In the beginning, keep the puppy on-leash when you suspect that he will encounter a cat. The first time he sees the cat sunning herself on the grass, he will probably strain on his leash to reach her. Ignore the cat, disregard the pulling, and continue on to your destination. If it's time for the puppy to eliminate, focus on "go potty." Eventually, the puppy will copy your attitude and ignore the cat.

If you have an indoor rather than an outdoor cat, use the same process. Keep the puppy on-leash to prevent him from running wildly through the house chasing the cat. Use a waist leash to keep the puppy near you. If the puppy sees a cat and starts pulling in the cat's direction, walk with purpose past the cat, or in the opposite direction. Ignore potential prey. Stay calm. Redirect the puppy's attention to you by using previously taught behaviors such as "look," "sit," "down," or "leave it." In a few weeks, the puppy will pick up on your attitude and ignore the cat. (If you have a puppy that already chases cats, turn to page 152 to learn how to "buddy up." Turn to Chapter 20 to learn how to teach "look," "sit," "down," or "leave it.")

You can plan specific cat and puppy introduction sessions. After a puppy is physically and mentally tired, have someone hold the cat on her lap as you walk by with the puppy. Reward calm, quiet behavior and repeat. (Don't forget to reward the cat, too!)

Note: Cats have natural defenses against puppies. They hiss, bat, and use their claws to make pups leave them alone. If you are worried that your cat's nails might scratch a puppy's eyes, put nail caps on them until the puppy learns to respect the cat.

Herding dogs like border collies or German shepherds see trotting, running horses, and "know" they need a quick nip there, and a fast move here to speed them on their way. However, horses do not like to be herded by dogs. Do not allow it. A kick by a horse can seriously injure or kill a dog. Never permit a puppy to bark or run the fence line. Prevent chasing by keeping a puppy on-leash when you take walks near horses. If the puppy starts running toward the horses, walk in the opposite direction. Ignore potential prey. Stay calm. Redirect the puppy's attention to you by using previously taught behaviors such as "look," "sit," "down," or "leave it."

Do not allow the puppy's attitude toward cats, horses, squirrels, or rabbits to affect your disposition and conduct. As pack leader, teach the puppy to follow your example, ignore potential prey, and attend to the task at hand. When you know a puppy will listen to you, instead of following his instincts, the puppy earns off-leash privileges on your property and inside the house.

When your puppy meets other dogs who are not part of your pack, do not allow the dogs to immediately run free and play. Give them time to sniff, greet each other on-leash, and let them decide if they are compatible. Consider the size and attitude of the other dog before you allow your puppy to play with him.

One of my friends has a wonderful, friendly, adolescent, Belgian Tervuren. However, Bizbee plays rough. He runs, leaps, and pounces on top of other dogs. I've watched him play. I knew Jet could not handle Bizbee's super-physical approach to play until she was older. Jet and Bizbee met many times on-leash while we walked them together, but they were not allowed to run free. Last week Bizbee and Jet met for a play date in my front agility ring. Bizbee is twenty months old. Jet is thirteen months old. They ran, chased, and flew around the ring, a perfect match.

When dogs play with other dogs, they often sound loud and noisy, but that does not mean they are angry or churlish. Dogs often bark and yip when they play with each other. The only time Logan ever barks is when he plays with Red. It's a deep, low bark. He chases and dives at Red. Red runs away, but not too far; he wants to play with Logan. Red rolls on his back, belly up. Logan pounces on him. Then, they both leap up and run around the ring.

Watch your dog's behavior. Dogs pounce, run, and grab at each other in play. Mouth open, they bite "air," but not the other dog. The issue is not that dogs snap at each other. The question is how hard, injurious, or lethal is the bite or encounter? Red has a soft golden retriever mouth. Zoe places her muzzle inside his mouth, but Red does not bite down. Then, Zoe places her mouth around Red's muzzle, but she doesn't tighten her grip either. Neither dog exerts pressure. During play, dogs can run, chase, leap, pounce, bark, or yip. How they act depends on their playing style and their playmates. Do not interfere during play sessions, unless you see play becoming so rough that it can injure the puppy.

Note: Do not overreact. Hissing and growling is not aggression.

Puppies who meet a variety of dogs when they are young grow into friendly, social, and kind dogs. After the puppy settles into your family, it's time to meet new dogs. The best place to start is with friends, family members, and neighbors you know who have amiable and affable dogs. Chapter 22 describes how to hold a "yappy hour." Younger puppies can participate in a puppy kindergarten class. Older puppies can meet new dogs at doggy parks, condo common areas, or walks in the neighborhood.

As pack leader your responsibility is to be sensitive to the needs of your puppy and resident animals. Your actions and responses are pivotal in the creation of a smoothly running pack. When you plan ahead and act with awareness of canine, feline, and equine natures, you can raise a happy, friendly, social puppy who accepts you as leader, follows your example, and handles the presence of other animals successfully.

Chapter 25
Home Alone: Solitude Does Not Mean Loneliness

Friday nights at 7:00 P.M., the parking lot at Safeway is always packed with cars. Tonight is no exception. Maxine sighs as she drives into the lot. Her design students' final research projects cover the Honda's backseat. In the next two days, Maxine must review, analyze, and grade sixty-four magazine-spread strategies.

Shelby, Maxine's daughter, sits in the front seat talking about the experiment her class performed at the school playground. "Marcy and I climbed to the top of the jungle gym. I dropped a stone. Marcy dropped a feather. The class had to decide which object would hit the ground first." Maxine listens while Shelby chats about playground physics.

Maxine drives slowly through the lot, searching for a place to park. Suddenly Shelby quits talking, yelps, and points at the front of a row of cars. "Mommy, look at the puppies!" In the section reserved for handicapped parking, a man sits in front of an x-pen containing five black puppies. Each puppy has a different-colored ribbon tied around his neck. Pink, green, yellow, red, and blue ribbons trail down their shoulders. Shelby pulls on her mother's hand, excited to see the "rainbow dogs." Fifteen minutes later, Maxine buys the puppy with the yellow ribbon for fifty-five dollars.

At 8:30 A.M. on Monday morning, Maxine leaves Stetson, the new black puppy, outside in the backyard with a bowl of food and water while she goes to work.

At 5:30 P.M., Maxine returns home. As she walks from the garage to the house, Maxine sees one cushion from the new rattan outdoor furniture resting against the fence. Another cushion sits inside the flower garden. The rattan chair tilts at a crazy angle. Stetson had chewed off its leg. Maxine opens the door to the house and sees tiny dirt paw prints decorating the cream-colored carpet down the hallway.

Maxine follows the paw prints into Shelby's bedroom. Shelby and Stetson are lying on her white-flowered comforter. Maxine shouts at Shelby. "What were you thinking? You brought Stetson inside without cleaning his feet. Take him outside. There's dirt on the bed and the hallway carpet is filthy!"

Shelby carries Stetson outside. The door slams shut behind her. Stetson barks. Maxine heads for the kitchen for paper towels and cleaning solution.

At least once a month, I hear about a puppy who destroys, chews, defecates, urinates, digs, barks, or self-mutilates when left home alone. Puppies must learn how to balance play and rest, togetherness and separation, confinement and freedom, and choice and obedience.

Teach your puppy to be home alone by practicing short separation times *when you are at home*. Place the puppy in his dog den. Do not make a fuss over him. Leave. Remember, pack leaders come and go as they please. Then, vacuum carpets, wash clothes, or watch television. After you complete your task, take the puppy out of the dog den for a bathroom visit. Then, practice the greeting ritual. (Turn to Chapter 15 to review the greeting ritual.)

Dogs like dens. To create a "puppy retreat," designate a crate, x-pen, or small room as a puppy hideaway. Place a soft bed or rug, water dish, litter box, toys, bones, or balls inside the crate, x-pen, or laundry room. Toys and bones give the puppy something to play with or chew while they are confined. Change toys frequently to keep a puppy entertained.

Puppy hideaways give dogs a safe place to stay when you cannot supervise them. They are small private places where puppies retreat to eat, sleep, chew on a bone, or play with a toy. Place puppies inside a den to separate them from guests, activities, or situations that might be too intense, overwhelming, or harmful for puppies to handle safely.

My clients, Richard and Beth, invited twenty-six family members to celebrate Thanksgiving dinner and stay overnight during the long week-

Dogs like dens.

end. Realizing their house would be filled with toddlers and teenagers, they established different safe havens in the house and yard for Buffy, their twenty-six-week-old mastiff puppy. During the long weekend, Richard and Beth alternated Buffy's playtime with visits to the "puppy palaces."

Dog dens give puppies a place to chew a bone, relax, and sleep. Do not be surprised if a puppy seeks out his crate during the day. When we give bones to our dogs, Jet, the new puppy, runs to her crate to eat it. She knows the other dogs will respect her space. After running and playing, Zoe Samantha, our Doberman pinscher, curls up in her crate to rest and relax. Dogs enjoy having a place of their own.

Next, teach your puppy to be home alone by practicing short separation times *when you leave the house.* Place the puppy in his dog den. Do not make a fuss over him. Leave. When you return home, take the puppy out of his dog den for a bathroom visit. Then, practice the greeting ritual. Gradually increase the time a puppy is left alone. Remember, dog dens are temporary measures. After two hours, a young puppy needs time out of the dog den. If you cannot return home to care for the puppy, hire a pet sitter. Or, ask a friend, neighbor, or family member to take the puppy out for playtime, food, and a bathroom break. Prevent separation anxiety by teaching your puppy that separation is a temporary, not a permanent, condition.

Your role as pack leader curbs separation anxiety. Puppies who believe they are pack leader become frantic, upset, or destructive when you leave the house. However, if a puppy accepts you as pack leader, he accepts your decision to leave and waits peacefully for your return.

Jessica told me, "My puppy Jax knows when he's a bad dog. When I came home and saw one arm from my mother's antique teddy bear on the chair, its body on the carpet, and the head by the bedroom door, Jax slunk away. When I found him, his head sank between his front paws." Jessica thinks Jax looks guilty. I disagree. Jax felt her anger, retreated from it, and sent her canine calming signals.

Jax did not understand why Jessica shoved a broken bear in his face. He was unaware that the teddy bear was her mother's favorite toy as a child. Jessica had not taught Jax the difference between a teddy bear on her bed and stuffed dog toys.

Puppies make decisions every day. Never blame the puppy for chewing your shoes, lying on the couch, or digging up the garden if you have not spent time teaching him to make a different decision. Instead, help puppies make correct choices. It's easy. When you see the puppy chewing on his toy, praise him. When you see the puppy lying on the floor next to the couch, reward him.

Puppies learn quickly. A sixteen-week-old Sussex spaniel can live in a Philadelphia suburb with two children, a Chicago loft with three college roommates, or a five-acre ranchette in Grants Pass, Oregon, with you, your husband, and two pit bulls. However, suburban and country dogs have different schooling requirements: using doggy doors, riding in elevators, or avoiding rattlesnakes. Your responsibility is to work with a puppy's inner nature and raise a dog who understands how to live with a human pack.

Your task is to design schooling sessions that reinforce a puppy for making a correct choice.

Teach "get it" and "leave it" so puppies will not devour your mother's teddy bear, chew on the rug, or eat the couch cushions when they are left home alone. For example, during a schooling session, play with the puppy and her favorite toy. Set the toy on the floor three feet away from an item that you never want the puppy to chew, such as a shoe or glove. Tell the puppy to "get your toy." When she picks up the toy, click and treat. If the puppy makes an incorrect choice and runs to pick up the shoe, tell her "leave it." When she does, C/T. Then, move the toy and shoe closer together. Always reward the puppy when she chooses the toy. Repeat until the shoe and toy are next to each other, and the puppy consistently chooses the toy. During future sessions, replace the shoe with previously chewed shoes, gloves, or other items that the puppy must learn not to chew. (Turn to pages 207–208 to review how to teach "get it" and "leave it.")

"Tranquility is the master of agitation."[20]

Before you leave a puppy home alone for an extended period of time, tire him out mentally and physically. Take him for a walk. Have the puppy play "follow the leader" while you change tempo, directions, and gaits. Play ball and require that a puppy perform a "sit-stay" until you release her to get the ball. After puppies play, exercise, and work, they rest.

Give puppies a job when they are home alone. Hide four Kongs stuffed with dried liver treats, kibble, or peanut butter in the laundry room for the puppy to find. Fill a Buster Cube or Activity Ball with kibble for puppies to roll, push, and shove. Kongs, Buster Cubes, and Activity Balls are interactive toys that mentally stimulate and engage a puppy's attention as they work to empty it of kibble or treats. They instantly reward puppies

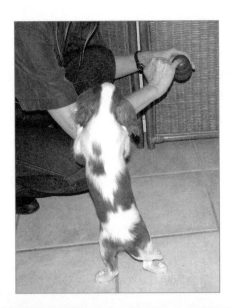

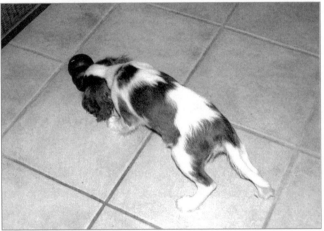

A Kong entertains a puppy.

for playing with them. Interactive toys give puppies alternatives to chewing on a doorjamb or eating your son's baseball mitt, and a puppy learns that solitude does not mean boredom or loneliness.

The way to "home alone" starts by creating a contented, peaceful puppy.

Afterword:
Raising a Puppy, Growing in Tao

Who has a genuine abundance to give to the world?
Only a person of Tao.[21]

I refuse to live in a world without puppies, tiny ambassadors of tao. In a busy world filled with heartaches and headaches, deadlines and commitments, furry representatives of tao remind me to play and look at things in a new way. With fresh eyes, I can see the natural unfolding of a mysterious process.

Followers of tao recognize there is more than one answer and more than one path but need help in finding the way. In raising puppies, we expose ourselves to the active presence of tao in our lives. Our small, furry tao instructors teach us the importance of listening to an inner voice, searching for an internal answer, and practicing abundance. Abundantly giving of ourselves to a new puppy's life. Opening ourselves to a border collie's curiosity as she explores the books, bags, and rocks that lie on the second-floor landing. Watching as an Irish setter digs through soft, fresh, loamy, black dirt to commune with ants, lizards, flowers, and trees.

Running through the gold, russet, and henna leaves of autumn or the madcap dash through lawn sprinklers, a Labrador retriever seizes the day and grabs our hearts. No shadows here. And we, the puppy's caregivers—if we are open, honest, and aware—are allowed to participate and experience the feel of tao, which is as close as the touch of a soft moist nose against our cheek.

We need puppies to remind us to be mindful during daily life as we wash dishes, eat bananas, walk to the mailbox, or play ball. Puppies do not take anything for granted. We must pay full attention or the banana bread that we left cooling on the counter may suddenly disappear, never to be seen again.

Puppies allow us to experience the immediacy of life and not let it pass us by without recognition. Our inner wisdom grows as we look and listen for tao teachings. Puppies teach us the meaning of following a "practice." A practice of devotion, imagination, serenity, and playfulness that serves us well in the rest of our life.

Words cannot describe tao. But puppies, in their infinite ability to teach us, reveal tao and show us the way to joy.

And for that, I am forever grateful.

Bibliography

Beaver, Bonnie V. *Canine Behavior: A Guide for Veterinarians*. Philadelphia: W. B. Saunders Co., 1999.

Book, Mandy and Cheryl S. Smith. *Quick Clicks: 40 Fast and Fun Behaviors to Train with a Clicker*. Carlsborg, WA: Hanalei Pets, 2001.

Cantrell, Krista. *Catch Your Dog Doing Something Right: How to Train Any Dog in Five Minutes a Day*. Guilford, CT: The Lyons Press, 2004.

——. *Housetrain Your Dog Now*. New York: Plume, 2000.

Dodds, W. Jean. E-mail to Krista Cantrell. 11 April 2004.

Feng, Gia-Fu and Jane English. *Lao Tzu: Tao Te Ching*. New York: Random House, 1972.

Fox, Michael W. *Behavior of Wolves, Dogs and Related Canids*. New York: Harper and Row, 1971.

Mammato, Bobbie. *Pet First Aid*. St. Louis: Mosby, 1997.

Rugaas, Turid. *On Talking Terms with Dogs: Calming Signals*. Legacy by Mail, 1997.

Scott, John Paul and John L. Fuller. *Genetics and the Social Behavior of the Dog*. Chicago: University of Chicago Press, 1965.

Walker, Brian Browne. *The Tao Te Ching of Lao Tzu*. New York: St. Martin's Press, 1995.

Endnotes

1. Brian Browne Walker, *The Tao Te Ching of Lao Tzu.* (New York: St. Martin's Press, 1995).

2. Ibid., Chapter 10.

3. Ibid., Chapter 49.

4. Gia-Fu Feng et al., *Lao Tzu: Tao Te Ching.* (New York: Random House, 1972).

5. Brian Browne Walker, *The Tao Te Ching of Lao Tzu.*

6. Ibid., Chapter 27.

7. Gia-fu Feng et al., *Lao Tzu: Tao Te Ching,* Chapter 14.

8. Brian Browne Walker, *The Tao Te Ching of Lao Tzu,* Chapter 22.

9. Ibid., Chapter 48.

10. Ibid., Chapter 7.

11. Ibid., Chapter 22.

12. Ibid., Chapter 51.

13. Ibid., Chapter 54.

14. Ibid., Chapter 44.

15. Ibid., Chapter 17.

16. Ibid., Chapter 65.

17. Gia-fu, Feng et al., *Lao Tzu: Tao Te Ching,* Chapter 77.

18. Brian Browne Walker, *The Tao Te Ching of Lao Tzu,* Chapter 60.

19. Ibid., Chapter 30.

20. Ibid., Chapter 26.

21. Ibid., Chapter 77.

Index